LEISURE ARTS PRESENTS

THE SPIRIT OF CHRISTMAS

CREATIVE HOLIDAY IDEAS BOOK FIVE

Christmas is a time for remembering — both the first Noel of so long ago and our own cherished childhood celebrations. As we look back for a brief time each year, we recapture the joy of those days when we first began to understand the true spirit of Christmas. Inspired by our fond recollections, we reflect upon the age-old message of love, hope, and peace. And with childlike enthusiasm, we seek to convey these same wonderful feelings to the people around us. To help you proclaim your own glad tidings of the season, we've created this special book. It is our hope that it will enrich not only your life but also the lives of those you love. As you open your heart to the spirit of giving once again, may you find the same delight you knew as a child.

LEISURE ARTS, INC.
Little Rock, Arkansas

THE SPIRIT OF CHRISTMAS

BOOK FIVE

''...and it was always said of him, that he knew how to keep Christmas well, if any man alive possessed the knowledge. May that be truly said of us, and all of us!''

— From *A Christmas Carol* by Charles Dickens

EDITORIAL STAFF

Editor: Anne Van Wagner Childs
Executive Director: Sandra Graham Case
Creative Art Director: Gloria Bearden
Executive Editor: Susan Frantz Wiles

PRODUCTION:
Managing Editor: Sherry Taylor O'Connor
Project Coordinators: Kathy R. Bradley, Diana Heien Suttle, Dawn R. Kelliher, Nancy L. Taylor, and Ginger A. Alumbaugh
Design Coordinator: Patricia Wallenfang Sowers
Foods Editor: Susan Warren Reeves, R.D.
Contributing Foods Editor: Christy Kalder

EDITORIAL:
Associate Editor: Dorothy Latimer Johnson
Senior Editorial Writer: Linda L. Trimble
Editorial Writer: Laurie R. Burleson
Editorial Copy Assistants: Tammi Williamson-Bradley, Holly Leigh Sell, Darla Burdette Kelsay, Marjorie Lacy Bishop, Sherry L. Lloyd, and Tena Kelley Vaughn
Advertising and Direct Mail Senior Copywriter: Eva M. Delfos

ART:
Production Art Director: Melinda Stout
Senior Production Artist: Linda Lovette
Art Production Assistants: Leslie Loring Krebs, Susan M. Vandiver, and Cindy Zimmerebner
Photography Stylists: Karen Smart Hall, Jan Vinsant, and Judith Howington Merritt
Typesetters: Cindy Lumpkin and Stephanie Cordero
Advertising and Direct Mail Artists: Sondra Harrison Daniel and Kathleen Murphy

BUSINESS STAFF

Publisher: Steve Patterson
Controller: Tom Siebenmorgen
Retail Sales Director: Richard Tignor
Retail Marketing Director: Pam Stebbins
Retail Customer Services Director: Margaret Sweetin
Marketing Manager: Russ Barnett
Executive Director of Marketing and Circulation: Guy A. Crossley
Fulfillment Manager: Scott Sharpe
Print Production: Nancy Reddick Lister and Laura Lockhart

International Standard Book Number 0-942237-11-0

TABLE OF CONTENTS

THE SIGHTS OF CHRISTMAS

Page 6

TABLE OF CONTENTS
(Continued)

THE SHARING OF CHRISTMAS

Page 88

THE TASTES OF CHRISTMAS

Page 110

HOLIDAY MORNING BRUNCH ..128

CAROLING PARTY 134

SANTA'S SWEETSHOP 142

GIFTS FROM THE KITCHEN........150

GENERAL INSTRUCTIONS 156

CREDITS 158

THE SIGHTS OF CHRISTMAS

Christmas is a time when we can transform our surroundings in a wonderfully magical way. With a fanciful theme and a few well-chosen decorations, we can create a delightful atmosphere — one that makes entering our homes just like stepping into fairyland. What better gift to offer family and friends than such a festive haven! Surrounded by treasured keepsakes and charming new creations, we find great joy in our Christmas celebration.

WINTER IN THE VILLAGE

In years gone by, the first snow of winter brought a flurry of activity to the frontier village. As each starry evening brought Christmas closer, lights twinkled in every window while busy hands made preparations for the coming season. The simple handmade decorations reflected both life in the village and the artistic talents of everyday people.

Here, a collection of old-fashioned ornaments captures the charm of holidays past. High atop the tree, a felt man in the moon watches over a settlement of "log" cabins and a gathering of stuffed muslin snowmen. Tiny white lights and snowy accents enhance the wintry look of the tree, and coordinated fabrics are used to create a homey atmosphere throughout the room. Above the mantel, an appliquéd wall hanging pictures a nighttime scene from the sleepy town. A strip of paper icicles provides a frosty setting for a little village, and handmade stockings await Santa's arrival.

Instructions for the projects shown here and on the next four pages begin on page 14. This year, why not create your own little Christmas village!

The **Starry Tree Skirt** *(page 17)* has a light sprinkling of appliquéd stars and a colorful triangle edging adapted from an antique quilt border. Fabric bows and nostalgic trimmings give a homey air to brown paper packages.

(Below) Nestled in a cluster of ''snowy'' **Rag Strip Trees** *(page 14)*, a trio of **Pretzel Log Cabins** *(page 18)* makes a cozy arrangement.

(Opposite) Tucked among the branches of the **Wintry Village Tree** *(page 14)*, a community of **Pretzel Log Cabins** *(page 18)* is inhabited by muslin **Snowman Ornaments** *(page 16)*. Hand-shaped **Papier Mâché Star and Icicle Ornaments** *(page 15)* have an antique finish, and the **Rag Strip Garland** *(page 14)* is fashioned from coordinating fabrics. Snowy pinecones and fabric bows accented with jingle bells round out the handcrafted decorations.

Depicting a starry night, our appliquéd **Village Wall Hanging** *(page 19)* is displayed above a mantel trimmed with a **Paper Icicle Border** *(page 14)*. As on all the appliquéd projects in this collection, the "stitching" around each motif on the wall hanging is added with a felt-tip pen.

A friendly **Snowman Ornament** *(page 16)* waves from a basket of cottony **Snowballs** *(page 14)*, frosty pinecones, and sprigs of evergreen.

Encircled by an evergreen wreath, a **Pretzel Log Cabin** *(page 18)* lies warm and snug beneath an antiqued felt **Moon Treetop Ornament** *(page 20)* and **Papier Mâché Star Ornaments** *(page 15)*. A fabric bow with pewter jingle bells adds a bit of festive color.

These roomy stockings are edged with colorful triangles to match our tree skirt *(shown on page 11)*. The **Appliquéd Stocking** *(page 17)* echos the peaceful scene on the wall hanging, and the **Snowman Stocking** *(page 16)* features a folded cuff and a smiling snowman.

WINTRY VILLAGE TREE

(Shown on page 9)

Twinkling with purchased white miniature lights, the blue-green boughs of a seven-foot-tall tree provide the backdrop for a village of tiny cabins settling down for a snowy winter holiday. Keeping watch over the village is a friendly Moon Treetop Ornament (page 20) made from soft fuzzy felt. An assortment of homey fabrics creates a Rag Strip Garland (on this page) that forms a winding road around the tree. The snow-covered Pretzel Log Cabins (page 18) arranged along the garland path are carefully crafted by gluing pretzel sticks and oyster crackers to a tagboard base. Painted doors and windows finish each house. Dressed in warm scarves and hats, smiling muslin Snowman Ornaments (page 16) dance among the branches. Rustic Papier Mâché Star Ornaments (page 15) shine softly in the night. Like the stars, the Papier Mâché Icicle Ornaments (page 15) are formed by applying instant papier mâché over an aluminum foil form.

Gleaming in the moonlight, the snow on the branches of the pinecone "trees" is created by brushing Duncan Snow Accents™ on the tips of large pinecones. Bows formed from 2½" x 22" strips of fabric provide sounds of the season when 1" dia. pewter jingle bells are wired to the center of each one.

Even the Starry Tree Skirt (page 17) reflects a scene of a winter evening. Dark fabric is dusted with golden fabric stars, and each star is "stitched" in place with lines made by a felt-tip pen. A cheerful trim of fabric triangles edges the circular skirt.

PAPER ICICLE BORDER   (Shown on page 12)

You will need white butcher paper, small sharp scissors, tracing paper, graphite transfer paper, transparent tape, and removable tape.

1. Trace icicle border pattern onto tracing paper.
2. Cut a 4" x 15" length of butcher paper. Fold 1 short edge 3¾" to 1 side. Using fold as a guide, fanfold remaining length of paper. Use removable tape to tape edges of paper together so paper will not shift when cutting.
3. Matching solid straight edge of pattern to 1 short edge of folded paper,

use transfer paper to transfer pattern to folded paper.
4. Cut out paper along solid lines only. Unfold paper and use a warm, dry iron to remove fold lines.
5. Repeat Steps 2 — 4 for desired number of lengths. Use transparent tape to tape lengths together.

RAG STRIP TREES

(Shown on page 11)

For each tree, you will need a plastic foam cone (we used 6"h and 9"h cones), green spray paint, green print cotton or cotton-blend fabrics, 3-ply jute, thread to match fabrics, straight pins, and craft glue.

1. Shape top of cone with fingers, pressing foam firmly to form a point.
2. Spray paint cone; allow to dry.
3. Cut a 4" square from 1 fabric. Refer to **Fig. 1** and glue fabric over top of cone.

Fig. 1

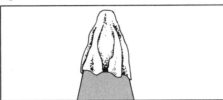

4. Cut a total of thirty-six 2½" x 6" pieces from different fabrics. Follow Steps 2 — 4 of Rag Strip Garland instructions on this page to make a 72" long rag strip. Trim jute at ends of rag strip.
5. Beginning 1" from bottom of cone, refer to **Fig. 2** and wind rag strip around cone, pinning to secure. Trim excess fabric at top of cone.

Fig. 2

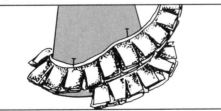

RAG STRIP GARLAND

(Shown on page 10)

You will need desired cotton or cotton-blend fabrics, 3-ply jute, and thread to match jute.

1. Cut fabrics into 5" x 6" pieces.
2. Matching edges, stack 3 fabric pieces together (we used a light, a medium, and a dark fabric). Alternating colors and fabrics, repeat with remaining fabric pieces.
3. Beginning 12" from end of jute, center jute between long edges on top of 1 stack of fabrics. Using a medium width zigzag stitch with a medium stitch length, sew jute to fabric pieces. With short edges of fabric stacks meeting (**Fig. 1**), repeat to sew jute across each fabric stack to form desired length of garland. Cut jute 12" from end of garland.

Fig. 1

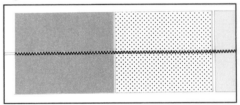

4. At approximately ½" intervals, clip ¼" into long edges of each fabric piece, staggering clips as shown in **Fig. 2**. At each clip, tear fabric up to zigzag-stitched line.

Fig. 2

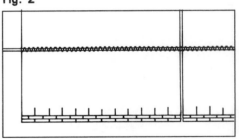

SNOWBALLS

(Shown on page 12)

For each snowball, you will need aluminum foil, cotton batting, and craft glue (optional).

1. Crumple aluminum foil into a firm ball approximately 2½" in diameter.
2. Tear 1" wide strips from cotton batting. Wrap batting strips around foil ball, slightly overlapping long edges. If necessary, use craft glue to secure batting.

PAPIER MÂCHÉ STAR AND ICICLE ORNAMENTS (Shown on page 10)

For each ornament, you will need 1 approx. 2" long bobby pin; aluminum foil; instant papier mâché (we used Celluclay® Instant Papier Mâché; a 1 lb. package will make approx. 50 ornaments); resealable plastic bag (optional); gesso; white, ivory, or dk gold acrylic paint; matte clear acrylic spray; dk brown waterbase stain; foam brushes; and a soft cloth.

STAR ORNAMENT

1. (Note: For Steps 1 — 5, use measurements given as general guidelines.) Refer to **Fig. 1a** to bend prongs of bobby pin to form an approximately 45 degree angle. To form bottom points of star, use approximately 6" squares of aluminum foil and wrap and crush foil pieces firmly around bent prongs of bobby pin (**Fig. 1b**).

Fig. 1a

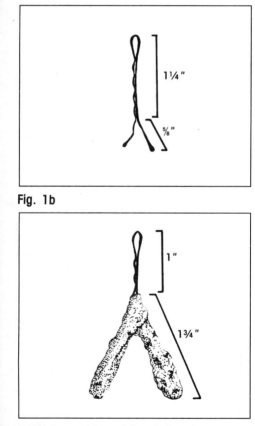

Fig. 1b

2. To form side points of star, form a 4" long roll of foil ¼" in diameter; wrap roll around center of bobby pin (**Fig. 2**).

Fig. 2

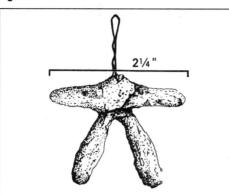

3. To form top point of star, wrap and crush a small piece of foil around top of bobby pin, leaving top ¼' of bobby pin exposed for hanger. Wrap additional pieces of foil around star as needed to fill out shape. Foil star should be well shaped and firm before papier mâché is added (**Fig. 3**).

Fig. 3

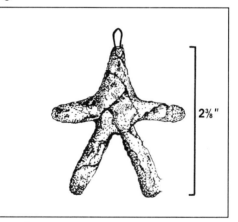

4. Following manufacturer's instructions, mix papier mâché with water (Excess mixture can be stored in a plastic bag in refrigerator for up to 4 days.)

5. Apply a ¼" to ½" thick layer of papier mâché over foil star, smoothing papier mâché with palms and forming points of star with fingers.

6. Hang star to dry, allowing papier mâché to dry overnight or until hard and dry.

7. Apply 1 coat of gesso to star; allow to dry. Paint star ivory or dk gold; allow to dry. Spray star with acrylic spray; allow to dry.

8. Apply stain to star and remove excess with soft cloth; allow to dry.

9. Spray star with acrylic spray; allow to dry.

ICICLE ORNAMENT

1. Separate prongs of bobby pin slightly (**Fig. 4**).

Fig. 4

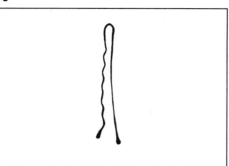

2. (Note: For Steps 2 and 3, use measurements given as general guidelines.) Leaving top ¼" of bobby pin exposed for hanger, wrap and crush an 8" square of foil firmly between and around prongs, forming an icicle shape. Wrap additional pieces of foil around icicle as needed to fill out shape. Foil icicle should be well shaped and firm before papier mâché is added (**Fig. 5**).

Fig. 5

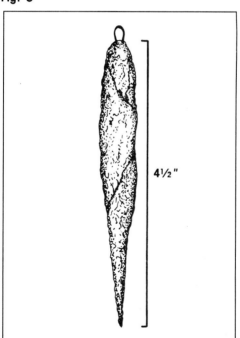

3. Follow Steps 4 — 6 of Star Ornament instructions to apply papier mâché to icicle.

4. Using white paint to paint icicle, follow Steps 7 — 9 of Star Ornament instructions to complete icicle.

SNOWMAN ORNAMENTS

(Shown on pages 10 and 12)

For each snowman, you will need two 5" x 8" pieces of unbleached muslin for snowman; one 5" x 6" piece of black felt for hat; one ½" x 9" fabric strip for scarf; thread to match muslin and felt; tracing paper; removable fabric marking pen; small crochet hook (to turn fabric); polyester fiberfill; 6 small rocks for eyes, nose, and buttons (we used approx. ³⁄₁₆"w rocks; rock for nose is slightly pointed); black and orange acrylic paint; paintbrushes; red embroidery floss; heavy thread (buttonhole twist); two approx. 2¾" long twigs for arms; hot glue gun; glue sticks; and seam ripper.

1. Paint rock for nose orange; paint remaining rocks black. Allow to dry.
2. Use snowman pattern and follow **Transferring Patterns** and **Sewing Shapes**, page 156, to make snowman from muslin pieces. Stuff snowman with fiberfill; sew final closure by hand.
3. To make indentations for eyes, nose, and buttons, use heavy thread to come up through snowman at 1 ●; go down through snowman ⅛" away. Pull thread tightly to create a dimple in snowman; knot thread and trim ends. Repeat for remaining ●'s.
4. Referring to photo, glue rocks to snowman. Use 2 strands of floss and Running Stitch, page 156, to work mouth.
5. For arms, refer to photo, page 12, and use seam ripper to make a ¼" opening at each side of snowman. Apply glue to 1 end of each twig and insert twigs into openings.
6. For hat, trace top, side, and brim patterns onto tracing paper and cut out. Use patterns and cut hat pieces from felt.
7. For hat side piece, match short edges and whipstitch short edges together to form a tube. Whipstitch hat top to 1 edge of hat side piece. Whipstitch inner edge of hat brim to remaining edge of hat side piece.
8. Referring to photo, glue hat on head. Tie scarf fabric around neck.

SNOWMAN

HAT TOP
(cut 1)

HAT BRIM

(cut 1)

HAT SIDE (cut 1)

SNOWMAN STOCKING

(Shown on page 13)

You will need two 12" x 18" pieces of fabric for stocking, two 12" x 22" pieces of fabric for lining and cuff, eight 4" squares of fabric for triangle edging on cuff, one 1½" x 5" piece of fabric for hanger, thread to match stocking and lining fabrics, tracing paper, fabric marking pencil, and 1 Snowman Ornament (on this page).

1. Matching registration marks (⊕) and overlapping pattern pieces, trace stocking pattern, page 37, onto tracing paper and cut out.
2. Leaving top edge open, use pattern and follow **Sewing Shapes**, page 156, to make stocking from fabric pieces.
3. For lining, extend top edge of pattern 3½" (**Fig. 1**); use fabric pieces and repeat Step 2. Do not turn right side out.

Fig. 1

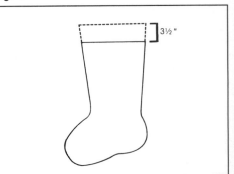

4. (**Note:** Use a ¼" seam allowance.) For triangle edging on lining, follow Step 5 of Starry Tree Skirt instructions, page 17, to make 8 triangles. Adjusting placement by overlapping edges if necessary, follow Steps 6 and 7 of Starry Tree Skirt instructions, page 17, to sew 4 triangles in first layer and remaining triangles in second layer. Press seam allowance toward lining.
5. Press top edge of stocking ½" to wrong side. With wrong sides facing, insert lining into stocking; tack lining to stocking at side seams. Turn top of lining to outside of stocking to form cuff.
6. For hanger, press all edges of fabric piece ¼" to wrong side. With wrong sides together, fold hanger piece in half lengthwise; press. Sew long edges together. Fold hanger in half to form a loop. Place ends of hanger inside completed stocking at heel side with approximately 2" of hanger extending above stocking; tack in place.
7. Refer to photo and tack snowman ornament to stocking.

APPLIQUÉD STOCKING

(Shown on page 13)

You will need two 12" x 18" pieces of fabric for stocking, two 12" x 18" pieces of fabric for lining, eight 4" fabric squares for triangle edging, one 1½" x 5" piece of fabric for hanger, fabric scraps for appliqués, thread to match stocking and lining fabrics, tracing paper, fabric marking pencil, paper-backed fusible web, and a black permanent felt-tip pen with fine point.

1. Matching registration marks (⊕) and overlapping pattern pieces, trace stocking pattern, page 37, onto tracing paper and cut out.
2. Leaving top edge open, use pattern and follow **Sewing Shapes**, page 156, to make stocking from fabric pieces.
3. For hanger, press long edges of fabric piece ¼" to wrong side. With wrong sides together, fold hanger piece in half lengthwise; press. Sew long edges together.
4. Fold hanger in half to form a loop. Matching raw edges of hanger to top raw edge of stocking, place hanger along seamline at heel side on right side of stocking; baste raw edges in place.
5. (**Note:** Use a ¼" seam allowance.) For triangle edging, follow Step 5 of Starry Tree Skirt instructions on this page to make 8 triangles. Adjusting placement by overlapping edges if necessary, follow Steps 6 and 7 of Starry Tree Skirt instructions on this page to sew 4 triangles in first layer and remaining triangles in second layer. Press seam allowance toward stocking.
6. For lining, use lining fabric pieces and repeat Step 2; do not turn right side out. Press top edge ¼" to wrong side.
7. With wrong sides together, insert lining into stocking and pin in place. Slipstitch lining to stocking.
8. To decorate stocking, trace moon, small star, house, house roof, house window, house door, small spruce, and spruce trunk patterns, pages 20 and 21, onto tracing paper and cut out. Referring to photo for placement, follow Steps 4 – 6 of Village Wall Hanging instructions, page 19.

STARRY TREE SKIRT   (Shown on page 11)

You will need two 45" squares of fabric for tree skirt, fabric scraps for triangle edging, fabric scraps for star appliqués, fabric marking pen, thumbtack or pin, string, thread to match tree skirt fabric, tracing paper, paper-backed fusible web, and a black permanent felt-tip pen with fine point.

1. For tree skirt, fold 1 fabric square in half from top to bottom and again from left to right.
2. To mark outer cutting line, tie 1 end of string to fabric marking pen. Insert thumbtack through string 22" from pen. Insert thumbtack in fabric as shown in **Fig. 1** and mark ¼ of a circle.

Fig. 1

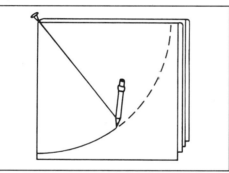

3. To mark inner cutting line, repeat Step 2, inserting thumbtack through string 2" from pen.
4. Cut out skirt along marked lines. For opening in back of skirt, cut along 1 fold from outer to inner edge.
5. For triangle edging, cut a 4" square from a fabric scrap. Fold square in half from top to bottom. Fold side edges to meet long raw edge, forming a triangle (**Fig. 2**); press. Repeat to make a total of 71 triangles.

Fig. 2

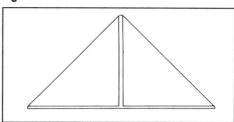

6. Matching raw edges and making sure bottom points of triangles meet (**Fig. 3**), baste 1 layer of triangles along outer edge on right side of tree skirt.

Fig. 3

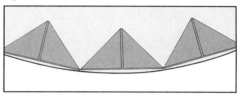

7. Referring to **Fig. 4**, baste a second layer of triangles to skirt on top of first layer.

Fig. 4

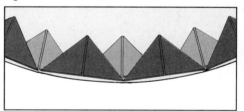

8. To line skirt, place skirt and remaining fabric square right sides together; pin in place. Leaving an opening for turning, sew ½" from all raw edges of skirt. Using raw edge of skirt as a guide, cut away excess lining fabric. Clip seam allowance and cut corners diagonally. Turn right side out; press. Sew final closure by hand.
9. For star appliqués, trace star patterns on this page onto tracing paper and cut out.
10. Cut a piece of web slightly smaller than each star fabric scrap. Follow manufacturer's instructions to fuse web to wrong side of each fabric scrap. Use patterns and cut out desired number of stars.
11. Referring to photo, fuse stars to tree skirt. Use felt-tip pen to draw lines on edges of stars to resemble stitches.

PRETZEL LOG CABINS (Shown on page 10)

For each cabin, you will need one 8½" x 11" piece of tagboard (manila folder), tracing paper, ruler, approx. 2½" long straight pretzels, oyster crackers, bite-size shredded wheat cereal, black acrylic paint, small flat paintbrushes, matte clear acrylic spray, and Design Master® glossy wood tone spray, Duncan Snow Accents™, and Bond™ 527 Multi-purpose Cement (available at craft or hobby stores).

1. Matching registration marks (⊕) and overlapping pattern pieces, trace cabin pattern onto tracing paper and cut out.
2. Use pattern and cut 1 cabin from tagboard. Place ruler against each fold line (indicated by dotted lines on pattern) and fold tagboard to form walls of cabin. For roof, cut one 3½" x 5" piece from tagboard. Matching short edges, fold roof in half.
3. (**Note:** Follow manufacturer's instructions when gluing with cement.) Overlap cabin wall and flap; glue to secure.
4. Lightly spray cabin and roof with wood tone spray; allow to dry.
5. (**Note:** Refer to photo for Steps 5 – 11.) Beginning at bottom of each wall and breaking pretzels to fit

when necessary, glue pretzels to cabin (**Fig. 1**).

Fig. 1

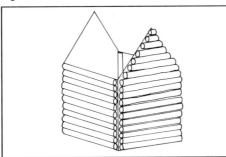

6. Glue 1 pretzel at each corner of cabin (**Fig. 2**).

Fig. 2

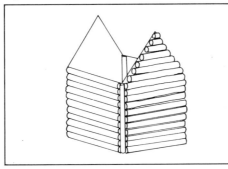

7. Glue roof to cabin.
8. For shingles, begin with bottom row on each side of roof and refer to **Fig. 3** to glue oyster crackers to roof.

Fig. 3

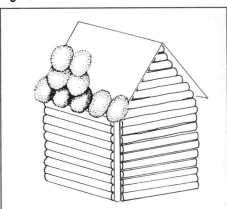

9. For chimney, glue 4 pieces of cereal together along long edges; glue chimney to roof.
10. Paint windows and doors black; allow to dry.
11. Apply Snow Accents™ to cabin; allow to dry.
12. Apply 2 coats of acrylic spray to cabin, allowing to dry between coats.

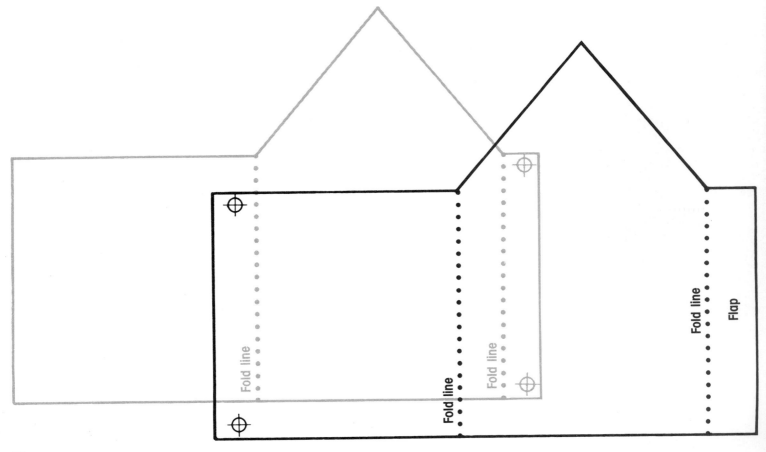

Fold line
Fold line
Fold line
Fold line
Flap

VILLAGE WALL HANGING (Shown on page 12)

You will need fabrics for wall hanging front (refer to photo for colors and fabric key for amounts), one 17¼" x 35" piece of muslin for background facing, one 21¼" x 39" piece of muslin for backing, one 1½" x 36" piece of muslin for hanging sleeve, 2 yds of 22"w paper-backed fusible web, thread to match border fabrics and muslin, tracing paper, 36" of ½" dia. wooden dowel, and a black permanent felt-tip pen with fine point.

1. Cut a piece of web slightly smaller than each background fabric piece. Follow manufacturer's instructions to apply web to wrong sides of fabric pieces.
2. Refer to **Fig. 1** to layer background fabric pieces on background facing fabric, overlapping ¼" where indicated by grey lines; fuse in place.

Fig. 1

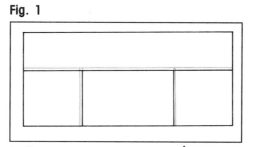

3. Trace wall hanging appliqué patterns, pages 20 and 21, onto tracing paper and cut out.
4. For appliqués, cut a piece of fusible web slightly smaller than each fabric scrap. Follow manufacturer's instructions to apply web to wrong sides of fabrics.
5. Use patterns and refer to Diagram to cut shapes from fabric scraps. Refer to Diagram and photo to position shapes on background; fuse in place.

6. Referring to photo, use pen to draw lines around shapes and background pieces to resemble stitches.
7. (**Note:** Use a ¼" seam allowance throughout.) Matching right sides and raw edges, refer to Diagram and sew side borders then top and bottom borders to background; press seams open.
8. Matching right sides and raw edges and leaving an opening for turning, sew backing to wall hanging front. Cut corners diagonally and turn right side out; press. Sew final closure by hand.
9. For hanging sleeve, press short edges of fabric ½" to wrong side and stitch in place. Press long edges ¼" to wrong side and stitch in place. With right side up, center 1 long edge of sleeve along top edge on backing; whipstitch sleeve to backing along long edges. Insert dowel in sleeve.

DIAGRAM

FABRIC KEY
- ■ Sky Background — One 6¾" x 35" piece
- ■ Center Background — One 10¾" x 16½" piece
- ■ Left Background — One 10¼" x 10¾" piece
- ■ Right Background — One 8¾" x 10¾" piece
- □ Appliqués — Fabric scraps
- ■ Side Borders — Two 2½" x 17¼" pieces
- ■ Top and Bottom Borders — Two 2½" x 39" pieces

Patterns on pages 20 and 21

MOON TREETOP ORNAMENT (Shown on pages 9 and 13)

You will need two 14" squares of gold felt (100% wool or wool blend), instant coffee, polyester fiberfill, thread to match felt, tracing paper, fabric marking pencil, small crochet hook (to turn fabric), cosmetic blush, 9" of florist wire, 6" of nylon line, and 1 Papier Mâché Star Ornament (page 15).

1. (**Note:** Wear rubber gloves when handling wet felt to protect hands from dye. After drying felt in dryer, wipe out dryer with a damp cloth to remove any dye residue.) To give felt the look of boiled wool fabric, place felt in boiling water for 1 minute; remove from water and allow to cool. Squeeze to remove excess water; dry in dryer.
2. Dissolve 1 tablespoon of instant coffee in 1 cup of hot water; allow to cool. Soak felt in coffee several minutes; remove from coffee and lay flat to dry.
3. Use moon treetop ornament pattern and follow **Transferring Patterns** and **Sewing Shapes**, page 156, to make moon from felt pieces. Stuff moon with fiberfill; sew final closure by hand.
4. Refer to photo and apply blush to cheek area on front of moon.
5. Refer to photo and use nylon line to hang star 1¼" from tip of moon.
6. Wire ornament to top of tree.

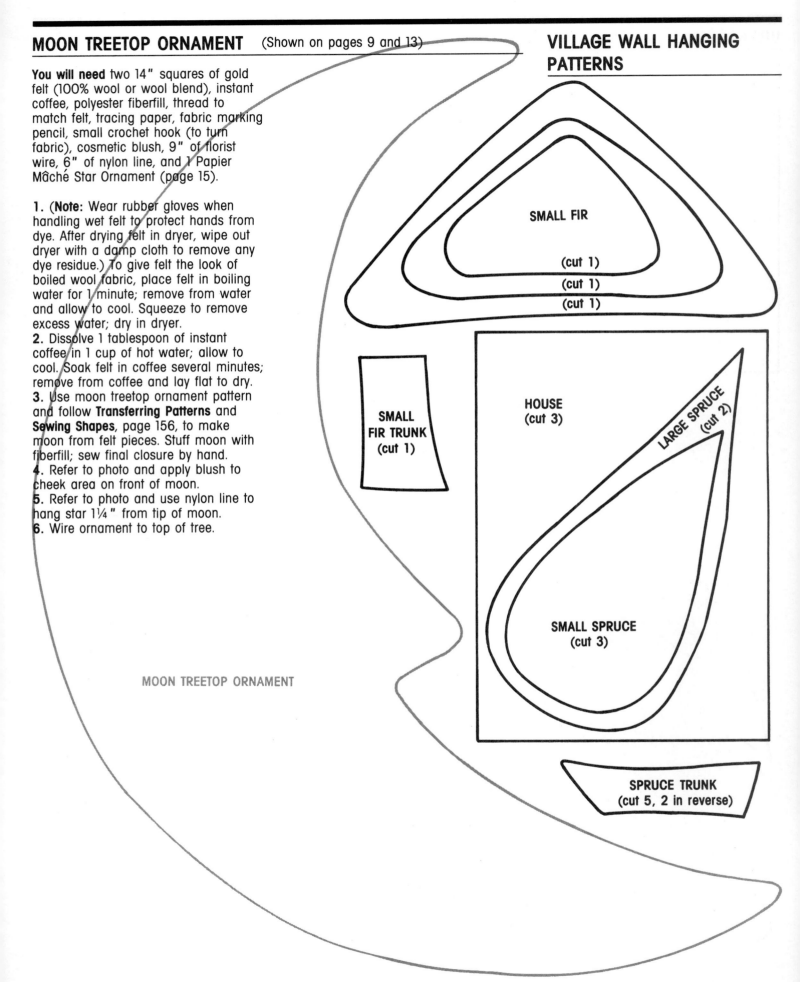

MOON TREETOP ORNAMENT

VILLAGE WALL HANGING PATTERNS

SMALL FIR

(cut 1)
(cut 1)
(cut 1)

SMALL FIR TRUNK (cut 1)

HOUSE (cut 3)

LARGE SPRUCE (cut 2)

SMALL SPRUCE (cut 3)

SPRUCE TRUNK (cut 5, 2 in reverse)

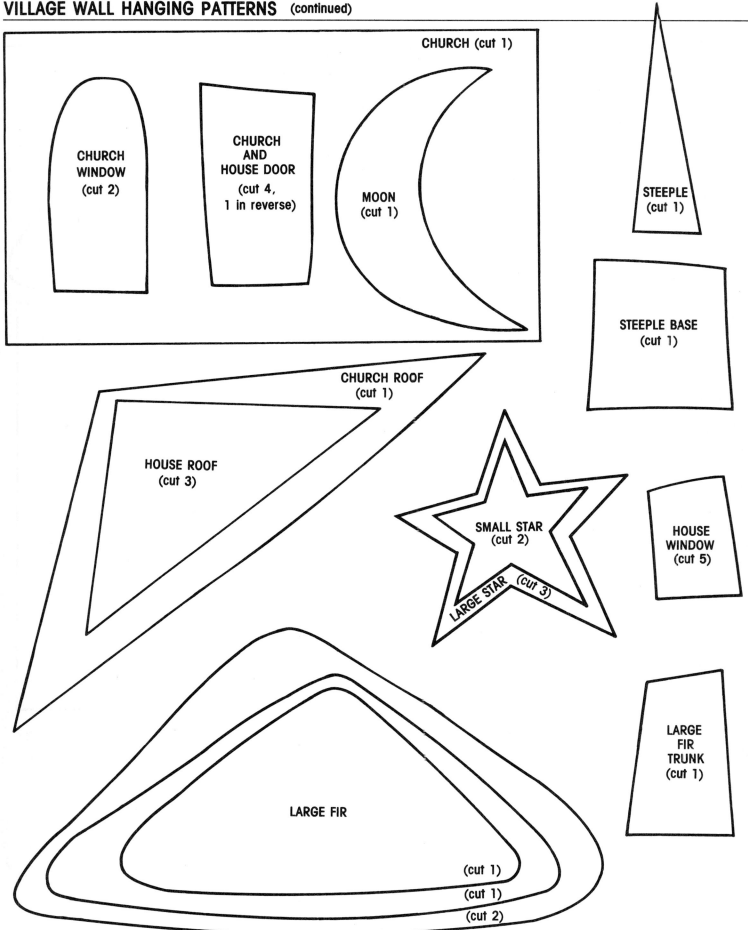

CHURCH (cut 1)

CHURCH WINDOW (cut 2)

CHURCH AND HOUSE DOOR (cut 4, 1 in reverse)

MOON (cut 1)

STEEPLE (cut 1)

STEEPLE BASE (cut 1)

CHURCH ROOF (cut 1)

HOUSE ROOF (cut 3)

SMALL STAR (cut 2)

LARGE STAR (cut 3)

HOUSE WINDOW (cut 5)

LARGE FIR TRUNK (cut 1)

LARGE FIR

(cut 1)

(cut 1)

(cut 2)

CELEBRATE A ROCK 'N' ROLL CHRISTMAS

Remember when Rock 'n' Roll was young? Poodle skirts, ponytails, and saddle oxfords worn with bobby socks were the most fashionable attire for teenage girls. And the coolest guy in school drove a hot rod with shiny chrome trim and a pair of fuzzy dice dangling from the rearview mirror. After school, the whole gang could be found at the malt shop sipping sodas and dancing to the latest hits on the jukebox. Elvis was fast becoming the heartthrob of the generation, and Hula-Hoops® were all the rage.

Perfect for decorating a recreation room or anyplace where friends gather to have a good time, this unique collection captures the exuberance of those fun-filled days.

Instructions for the projects shown on these two pages begin on page 24. Have a rockin' Christmas!

(Opposite) From the perky polka-dotted bow at its top to the petticoated **Poodle Tree Skirt** *(page 27)* at its base, the **Rock 'n' Roll Tree** *(page 24)* is boppin' with colorful bits of memorabilia. Hot pink Hula-Hoops® make a nifty garland, while a striped ribbon "music staff" accompanies the silvery **Music Ornaments** *(page 24)*. Bright turquoise **Cool Car Ornaments** *(page 24)* go for spins among frothy **Ice Cream Soda Ornaments** *(page 24)* and dangling **Fuzzy Dice Ornaments** *(page 25)*. Tiny saddle oxfords dance around the tree to the music of **Rockin' Records** *(page 24)*, and glittery glass balls are tied with polka-dotted ribbons.

The swell **Poodle Stocking** *(page 26)* for gals and the **Polka-dot Stocking** *(page 26)* for guys harmonize with the poodle tree skirt and treetop bow.

ROCK 'N' ROLL TREE
(Shown on page 22)

You can bop 'til you drop making fun ornaments to decorate this Rock 'n' Roll Christmas Tree! Reminiscent of some of the favorite fads from the Fifties, these memorable decorations are an easy way to brighten your holiday decor.

Our seven-foot-tall artificial Noble fir is encircled with everyone's favorite toy — bright pink and white Hula-Hoops®. We used a saw to cut apart two hoops and placed them around the bottom third of the tree. We placed two more uncut hoops over the tree and crisscrossed them at the center. The smaller hoops at the top of the tree were formed by cutting approximately one-quarter of the circumference from two more hoops. The ends were overlapped and taped securely with duct tape. The small hoops were placed around the top third of the tree with the tape hidden at the back among the branches.

No tribute to the decade would be complete without lots of music. We used a 1½" wide black and white striped ribbon as a "music staff" garland that rocks and rolls around the tree. Whimsical Music Ornaments (on this page) made from plastic foam meat trays are glittery accompaniments to the ribbon garland. Ready for a sock hop, pink and turquoise Rockin' Records (on this page) are tucked among the branches.

Turquoise Cool Car Ornaments (on this page) take spins around the tree, and Fuzzy Dice Ornaments (page 25) would look right at home on a rearview mirror. If anyone dances up a thirst, the "strawberry" Ice Cream Soda Ornaments (on this page) look good enough to drink.

Purchased toddlers' saddle oxfords are sized just right for ornaments. Their black and white good looks are a Fifties classic that is still available today. And if bows on ponytails were all the rage then, a taffeta treetop bow is sure to be popular now. Tiny matching bows adorn glittery ball ornaments that are made by applying spray adhesive to glass balls and rolling them in glitter.

This "blast from the past" wouldn't be complete without a poodle skirt, so we created a Poodle Tree Skirt (page 27) complete with four prancing poodles wearing rhinestone collars. So turn on the jukebox and let your toes start tappin' around this fun and frolicking Rock 'n' Roll Tree.

ICE CREAM SODA ORNAMENTS
(Shown on page 22)

For each ornament, you will need 1 clear plastic juice-size drinking glass, pink acrylic paint, gesso, 6" of white cloth-covered florist wire, hot glue gun, glue sticks, foam brush, white tissue paper, two plastic drinking straws, medium mixing bowl, electric mixer, Ivory Snow™ laundry detergent, and 8" of nylon line (for hanger).

1. Mix 1 part paint to 1 part gesso. Paint inside of glass; allow to dry.
2. Bend wire in half to form a loop. With top of loop extending ½" above rim of glass, glue wire to inside of glass at 1 side.
3. Cut two 6½" lengths from straws. Refer to photo and place straws inside glass. Pack inside of glass with crumpled tissue paper to within ½" of rim to hold straws upright.
4. (**Note:** It may be necessary to add more detergent or water to whipped mixture to achieve correct consistency.) Mix 1 part detergent to 1 part water in bowl. Beat at highest speed of mixer for 4 to 7 minutes or until mixture resembles whipped cream.
5. Referring to photo, spoon whipped mixture into glass, covering tissue paper; allow to dry.
6. For hanger, thread nylon line through wire loop and knot ends of line together.

ROCKIN' RECORDS
(Shown on page 22)

For each record, you will need one 45 rpm phonograph record (we found ours at a local thrift store), gesso, pink or turquoise acrylic paint, foam brushes, craft glue, and silver glitter.

1. (**Note:** Follow Steps 1 – 3 for each side of record.) Apply 1 coat of gesso to record label; allow to dry.
2. Paint label pink or turquoise; allow to dry.
3. Apply a line of craft glue along outer edge of label; sprinkle glitter over glue, coating well. Allow to dry. Shake off excess glitter.

MUSIC ORNAMENTS
(Shown on page 22)

You will need plastic foam meat trays (available in meat department of grocery store), tracing paper, gesso, craft knife, foam brushes, craft glue, silver glitter, and nylon line (for hangers).

1. Trace music patterns onto tracing paper and cut out.
2. (**Note:** Follow Steps 2 – 5 for each ornament.) Place pattern on smooth side of tray and use a dull pencil to draw around pattern; use craft knife to cut out.
3. Apply 1 coat of gesso to ornament; allow to dry.
4. Apply a heavy coat of glue to top and sides of ornament; working quickly, sprinkle glitter over glue, coating well. Allow to dry. Shake off excess glitter.
5. For hanger, thread 8" of nylon line through top of ornament; knot ends of line together.

COOL CAR ORNAMENTS
(Shown on page 22)

For each ornament, you will need 1 approx. 5" x 8" plastic foam meat tray (available in meat department of grocery store); tracing paper; graphite transfer paper; craft knife; gesso; foam brush; turquoise, white, black, and lt grey acrylic paint; small round paintbrush; liner brush; craft glue; 1½" of 22-gauge florist wire; and silver glitter.

1. Trace car pattern, page 25, onto tracing paper.
2. (**Note:** For cars facing left, turn pattern over before transferring pattern to tray.) Use transfer paper and a dull pencil to transfer pattern onto smooth side of tray; use craft knife to cut out.
3. Apply 2 coats of gesso to ornament, allowing to dry between coats.
4. (**Note:** Refer to photo and color key for Steps 4 – 6.) Paint ornament; allow to dry.
5. For antenna, insert florist wire into edge of foam at back of car; glue to secure.
6. For "chrome", apply glue to car and antenna; sprinkle glitter over glue, coating well. Allow to dry. Shake off excess glitter.

COOL CAR ORNAMENTS (continued)

COLOR KEY
- ☐ white
- ☐ turquoise
- ☐ lt grey
- ■ black

FUZZY DICE ORNAMENTS (Shown on page 22)

For each ornament, you will need 1 approx. 2" x 4" piece of 1³⁄₁₆" thick plastic foam, paring knife, one 6" x 13" piece of turquoise sweatshirt fleece fabric, 8" of ¹⁄₁₆"w white satin ribbon, heavy white paper, tracing paper, hole punch, and craft glue.

1. Trace dice cover pattern onto tracing paper and cut out. Use pattern and cut 2 pieces from fleece.
2. Being careful to cut plastic foam very accurately, use knife to cut two 1³⁄₁₆" cubes.
3. Apply glue to 1 side of 1 cube. Refer to **Fig. 1** and place cube glue side down on smooth side of 1 cover piece; allow to dry.

Fig. 1

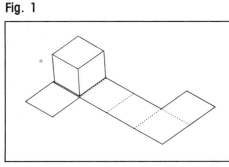

4. Apply glue to remaining sides of cube and wrap cover around cube, completely covering all sides.

5. Carefully lift up 1 corner of cover fabric and glue 1 end of ribbon to exposed foam (**Fig. 2**); glue corner of cover fabric over ribbon. Allow to dry. Trim excess fabric at seams if necessary.

Fig. 2

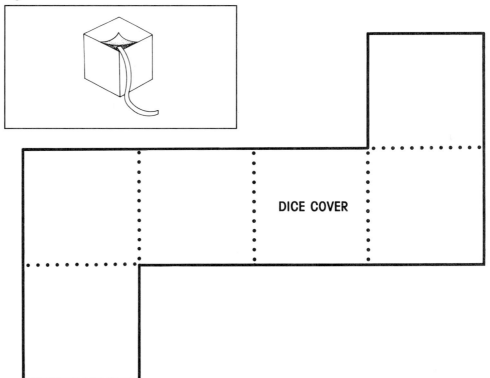

DICE COVER

6. Repeat Steps 3 – 5 for remaining foam cube, gluing remaining end of ribbon to cube.
7. Use hole punch to punch 42 dots from heavy paper; glue dots to each cube to resemble dice.

POODLE STOCKING (Shown on page 23)

You will need one 18" x 22" piece of pink felt; ⅝ yd of 72"w white nylon net fabric; one 8" x 10" piece of black felt; white, black, and pink thread; tracing paper; paper-backed fusible web; six ¾" dia. black pom-poms; ⅔ yd of ¹⁄₁₆" dia. silver metallic cord for leash; ⅞" of ⁵⁄₁₆"w double-strand rhinestone trim for collar (available at fabric stores); one 5mm turquoise sequin; one 2mm clear glass bead; fabric glue; and 5" of ⅛" dia. silver metallic cord for hanger.

1. Matching registration marks (⊕) and overlapping pattern pieces, trace stocking pattern, page 37, onto tracing paper and cut out.
2. Use pattern and cut 2 stocking pieces from pink felt. Matching edges and leaving top edge open, use a ⅜" seam allowance to sew stocking pieces together.
3. Cut four 5" x 72" strips from net. Matching edges, layer strips together. Matching short edges, fold strips in half. Using a ½" seam allowance, sew short edges together. Trim seam allowance to ⅛" and turn right side out.
4. To gather net, baste layers together ½" and ¼" from 1 raw edge. Pull basting threads, drawing up gathers to fit around top of stocking.
5. With gathered edge of net ⅝" from top edge of stocking, baste net to stocking (**Fig. 1**). Fold top edge of

stocking down ⅝", covering gathered edge of net. Stitch close to raw edge of felt.

Fig. 1

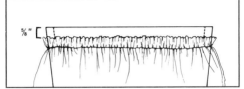

6. For poodle, trace poodle pattern onto tracing paper and cut out. Cut a piece of web slightly smaller than black felt; follow manufacturer's instructions to fuse web to felt. Referring to photo, use pattern and cut 1 poodle from felt.
7. (**Note:** Refer to photo for Steps 7 – 9.) Fuse poodle to stocking. Tack pom-poms to poodle where indicated by **x**'s on pattern; trim pom-poms on head into a smooth oval.
8. For leash, glue ¹⁄₁₆" dia. cord to poodle and stocking. For collar, glue rhinestone trim to neck of poodle over end of cord.
9. For eye, refer to pattern and sew sequin and bead to poodle.
10. For hanger, fold ⅛" dia. cord in half. Place ends of hanger inside stocking at heel side with approximately 1½" of loop extending above stocking; stitch in place.

POLKA-DOT STOCKING

(Shown on page 23)

You will need two 12" x 18" pieces of fabric for stocking, one 10" x 14" piece of white felt for cuff, 15" of ¼"w silver sequin trim, fabric glue, tracing paper, fabric marking pencil, thread to match fabric and felt, and 5" of ⅛" dia. silver metallic cord for hanger.

1. Matching registration marks (⊕) and overlapping pattern pieces, trace stocking pattern, page 37, onto tracing paper and cut out.
2. Place stocking fabric pieces right sides together and center stocking pattern on top. Use fabric marking pencil to draw around pattern; cut out stocking pieces.
3. (**Note:** Use a ½" seam allowance throughout.) With right sides facing and leaving top edge open, sew stocking pieces together. Trim seam allowance and clip curves.
4. For cuff, match short edges and fold felt in half. Sew short edges together; trim seam allowance. Matching wrong sides and long edges, fold felt in half. With wrong side of stocking and right side of cuff facing, match raw edges and sew cuff to stocking; trim seam allowance. Turn stocking right side out; fold cuff down over stocking.
5. Referring to photo, glue sequin trim around cuff ½" from bottom edge.
6. For hanger, fold silver cord in half. Place ends of hanger inside stocking at heel side with approximately 1½" of loop extending above stocking; stitch in place.

POODLE TREE SKIRT (Shown on page 22)

For tree skirt, you will need one 54" square of pink felt, one 11" x 32" piece of black felt, paper-backed fusible web, twenty-four ¾" dia. black pom-poms, 4" of ¼"w double-strand rhinestone trim for collars (available at fabric stores), 3 yds of 1/16" dia. silver metallic cord for leashes, four 5mm turquoise sequins, four 2mm clear glass beads, fabric glue, tracing paper, thumbtack or pin, fabric marking pencil, string, and black thread.

For petticoat, you will need one 50" square of white fabric (pieced as necessary), 9 yds of 72"w white nylon net fabric, white thread, and heavy thread (buttonhole twist).

TREE SKIRT

1. Fold pink felt in half from top to bottom and again from left to right.
2. To mark outer cutting line, tie 1 end of string to fabric marking pencil. Insert thumbtack through string 26" from pencil. Insert thumbtack in fabric as shown in **Fig. 1** and mark ¼ of a circle.

Fig. 1

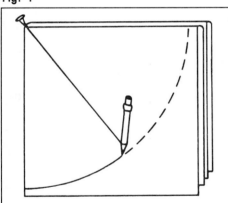

3. To mark inner cutting line, repeat Step 2, inserting thumbtack through string 2" from pencil.
4. Following cutting lines and cutting through all thicknesses of fabric, cut out skirt. For opening in back of skirt, cut along 1 fold from outer to inner edge.
5. Trace poodle pattern, page 26, onto tracing paper and cut out.
6. Cut a piece of web slightly smaller than black felt; follow manufacturer's instructions to fuse web to felt. Use pattern and cut 4 poodles from black felt.
7. Referring to Diagram, fuse poodles to skirt.
8. Tack pom-poms to each poodle where

indicated by **x**'s on pattern. Trim pom-poms on each head into a smooth oval.
9. For leashes, cut cord into four 27" lengths. Refer to Diagram and glue cord to poodles and skirt.
10. For collars, cut rhinestone trim into four 1" pieces; glue 1 piece to neck of each poodle over end of cord.
11. For eyes, refer to photo and pattern and sew 1 sequin and 1 bead to each poodle.

PETTICOAT

1. Inserting thumbtack through string 24" from pencil for outer cutting line, follow Steps 1 – 4 of Tree Skirt instructions to cut petticoat from white fabric.
2. Press inner edge of petticoat ¼" to wrong side, clipping curve as necessary; press ¼" to wrong side again and stitch in place.
3. Press each straight edge of petticoat ¼" to wrong side; press ¼" to wrong side again and stitch in place.
4. For net ruffle, cut net into thirty-two 10" x 72" strips. Matching edges, stack 4 strips together. Repeat with remaining strips to form a total of 8 stacks of net. Fold 1 stack in half lengthwise. Place

heavy thread on top of stack ½" from folded edge. Zigzag stitch over heavy thread, being careful not to stitch into thread. With short edges of fabric stacks meeting (**Fig. 2**), repeat to sew heavy thread across each stack to form 1 continuous length of net.

Fig. 2

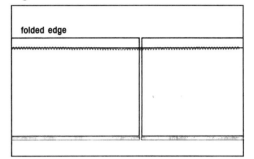

5. Pull heavy thread, drawing up gathers to fit outer edge of petticoat. Matching gathered edge of ruffle to raw edge of petticoat, pin ruffle to right side of skirt. Using a ⅝" seam allowance, sew ruffle to petticoat. Press seam allowance toward petticoat. Pull layers of net apart for fullness.
6. Place petticoat around base of tree. Arrange tree skirt on top of petticoat.

DIAGRAM

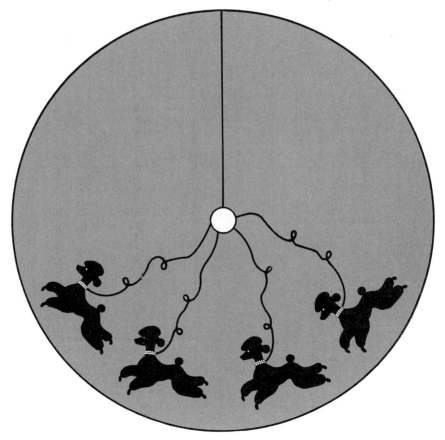

CHRISTMAS AT GRANDMOTHER'S HOUSE

Thoughts of Grandmother bring to mind a wealth of sentimental treasures. What child hasn't admired the flower-bedecked hats, elegant pearls, cameo brooches, and dainty white gloves found in Grandmother's cozy home — or discovered a nosegay of carefully pressed blossoms tucked away among scraps of ribbon and lace. Pretty handkerchiefs scented with rose water, snippets of embroidery, and delicately flowered teapots recall quiet afternoons spent at Grandmother's house.

Here we combine these genteel images to create a holiday collection filled with the grace of yesteryear. Instructions for the projects shown on these four pages begin on page 32.

This **Sentimental Wreath** (*page 32*) beautifully echoes the romance of bygone days.

(Opposite) Paying tribute to Grandmother's needlework skills, this **Sewing Box Centerpiece** *(page 33)* is all dressed up for the holidays with antique postcards and decorations from the tree. Sewn from floral print fabric, our **Handkerchief-Cuffed Stocking** *(page 36)* matches the feminine **Handkerchief Shelf Scarf** *(page 33)* shown on page 29.

(Right) Filled with fragrant potpourri, a **Rose Jar** *(page 33)* is adorned with a delicately stitched blossom.

(Bottom) A garland of lace and pearls accented with dainty **Nosegays** *(page 33)* encircles the **Grandmother's Tree** *(page 32)* with timeless beauty. Pretty handkerchiefs are made into **Floral Cone Ornaments** *(page 35)*, and flowery hats and scraps of embroidery are tucked among the branches. Classic **Cameo Ornaments** *(page 32)* and **Glove Bow Ornaments** *(page 32)* bring elegance to the tree while pink glass balls and ribbon-tied prisms lend holiday sparkle. Shown on page 29, a crocheted afghan makes a cozy tree skirt. Ours is an antique, but we've provided a pattern for the **Granny Square Afghan** *(page 34)* so that you can make your own.

GRANDMOTHER'S TREE
(Shown on page 29)

Warm memories of bygone days are found among the branches of our 7-foot-tall Grandmother's Tree. Pearls and lace, as well as gloves and old-fashioned hats, speak of quiet days of taking tea and playing dress-up in Grandmother's "old" clothes.

A garland of lace and pearls is created by draping purchased 2½" wide lace together with 2 strands of pearl bead garland. Covered florist wire is used to tie the strands in place on the branches. Accenting the garland are pretty Nosegays (page 33) made from silk and dried flowers.

Some of our flowery hats and some of the gloves for our Glove Bow Ornaments (on this page) were discovered in Grandmother's attic, and we added to our collection by shopping at flea markets and antique stores.

Pink glass balls and chandelier prisms reflect the twinkle in Grandmother's eyes. The prisms, which were found at an antique store, are given a feminine touch by hot-gluing bows of ¾" wide satin ribbon to their tops.

Tucked among the branches are purchased 4" diameter wooden embroidery hoops encircling pieces of old-fashioned embroidered dresser scarves and tea towels. We folded one edge of each embroidered piece to the front of the hoop and secured it with a needle threaded with embroidery floss.

Fashioned from cut paper inserted in purchased frames, classic Cameo Ornaments (on this page) grace the tree with timeless beauty. Lace, ribbons, and pretty handkerchiefs, which a lady in Grandmother's day was never without, are all combined to create Floral Cone Ornaments (page 35).

At the top of Grandmother's Tree is a larger version of a Nosegay made using wider ribbons. The lace and pearl garland, as well as a Glove Bow Ornament and an embroidery hoop, is arranged around the Nosegay to complete the top.

Used as a tree skirt, an antique afghan complements the sentimental decorations on our Grandmother's Tree. Using our Granny Square Afghan instructions (page 34), you can create your own afghan filled with warm memories of this holiday season.

CAMEO ORNAMENTS
(Shown on page 31)

For each ornament, you will need one 2¼" x 2¾" gold oval plastic frame with hanger, one 4" square of black drawing paper and one 3" square of cream drawing paper (available at art supply stores), 10" of ⅜"w satin ribbon, tracing paper, graphite transfer paper, craft knife, cutting mat or a thick layer of newspapers, rubber cement, and 6" of nylon line (for hanger).

1. Using cardboard frame back as a pattern, cut an oval from black paper. Place black oval on cardboard and insert in frame.
2. Trace cameo pattern onto tracing paper. Use transfer paper to transfer cameo to 1 side (wrong side) of cream paper.
3. Place cream paper wrong side up on cutting mat; use craft knife to cut out cameo.
4. Use rubber cement to glue cameo in center of frame.
5. Tie ribbon into a bow around hanger on frame; trim ends.
6. Thread nylon line through hanger and knot ends of line together.

SENTIMENTAL WREATH
(Shown on page 28)

You will need an 18" dia. artificial evergreen wreath, 3 Cameo Ornaments (on this page), 4 Nosegays (page 33; omit ribbon), 1 Glove Bow Ornament (on this page), lt green silk greenery, pearl bead garland, sprays of artificial white berries, hot glue gun, and glue sticks.

1. (**Note:** Refer to photo for Steps 1 – 3.) Insert silk greenery and berry sprays into wreath; glue to secure.
2. Glue glove bow, cameos, and nosegays to wreath.
3. Arrange garland on wreath; glue to secure.

GIFT WRAP
(Shown on page 29)

You will need lace-printed clear cellophane (available at florist shops), solid-colored gift wrap, transparent tape, desired widths of satin ribbon, and 1 Nosegay (page 33) or one 4" long chandelier prism.

1. Cut a piece of gift wrap large enough to wrap package. Cut a piece of cellophane the same size.
2. Place cellophane right side down on a flat surface; matching edges, place gift wrap right side down on top of cellophane. Center package on gift wrap and wrap package, using tape to secure seams and ends.
3. Referring to photo, tie lengths of ribbon around package into a bow. Use a short length of ribbon to tie nosegay or prism to bow.

GLOVE BOW ORNAMENTS
(Shown on page 31)

For each ornament, you will need 1 lady's wrist-length glove, 8" of 26-gauge wire, and thread to match glove.

1. Leaving thumb of glove free, fanfold glove lengthwise; wrap center securely with wire (**Fig. 1**).

Fig. 1

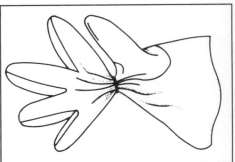

2. Wrap thumb around center of glove, covering wire; tack in place (**Fig. 2**).

Fig. 2

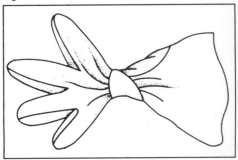

HANDKERCHIEF SHELF SCARF (Shown on page 29)

You will need handkerchiefs at least 8½" square (see Step 2 for number of handkerchiefs; we found our handkerchiefs at local antique stores and flea markets), white lightweight cotton fabric (see Step 1 for amount), removable fabric marking pen, tracing paper, ruler, and white thread.

1. For scarf measurements, measure length and width of shelf and add 1" to each measurement. Cut 2 pieces of fabric the determined measurements.
2. (**Note:** You will need 2 or 3 handkerchiefs for every 12" of scarf length; more than 1 corner can be cut from some handkerchiefs. For our 65½" long scarf, we used 15 handkerchief corners cut from 14 handkerchiefs.) For corner pattern, cut an 8½" square from tracing paper; cut square in half diagonally and discard 1 half.
3. Place pattern over desired corner of handkerchief, matching short edges of pattern to edges of handkerchief. Use fabric marking pen to draw a line on handkerchief along remaining edge of pattern. Cut handkerchief along pen line. Repeat for remaining handkerchiefs.
4. (**Note:** It may be necessary to adjust the amount of overlap on handkerchief corners to make corners fit scarf length.) Matching right sides and raw edges, refer to **Fig. 1** to pin 1 layer of handkerchief corners along 1 long edge of 1 fabric piece, overlapping handkerchief corners at least 1½".

Fig. 1

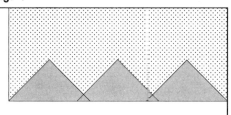

5. For each end of scarf, match finished edges and fold 1 handkerchief corner in half; press. Beginning and ending with a folded handkerchief corner pinned ½" from each short edge of fabric, refer to **Fig. 2** and repeat Step 4 to pin a second layer of handkerchief corners to fabric. Baste through all layers ½" from raw edge.

Fig. 2

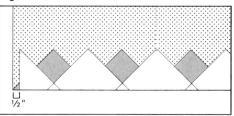

6. Matching right sides and raw edges, place fabric pieces together. Leaving an opening for turning and being careful not to catch folded edges of end handkerchief corners in seams on short edges, use a ½" seam allowance and sew pieces together. Turn right side out and press; sew final closure by hand. Remove any visible basting threads.

SEWING BOX CENTERPIECE (Shown on page 30)

You will need a sewing box (we found our 8" x 10" x 5½" box at a flea market), a block of floral foam to fit inside sewing box (block should be approx. 2" shorter than height of inside of box), artificial greenery, 2 antique postcards, 1 Glove Bow Ornament (page 32), 4 buttons, 3 glass ball ornaments, 1 Nosegay (on this page; omit ribbon), ⅔ yd of pearl bead garland, hot glue gun, and glue sticks.

1. (**Note:** Refer to photo for Steps 1 – 3.) Place foam inside box. Insert greenery into foam.
2. Glue buttons to glove bow. Glue bow to front of box.
3. Arrange postcards, glass ball ornaments, nosegay, and pearl garland in greenery; glue to secure.

NOSEGAYS (Shown on page 31)

For each nosegay, you will need 5 silk rosebuds, dried white baby's breath, dried plumosa fern, 24-gauge florist wire, wire cutters, and six 1 yd lengths of desired width satin ribbon in coordinating colors.

1. Referring to photo, insert rosebuds into a small cluster of baby's breath. Place dried fern around entire cluster. Wire all stems together. Trim stems 1" below wire.
2. Tie ribbon lengths together into a bow. Refer to photo and wire bow to bottom of cluster.

ROSE JAR (Shown on page 31)

You will need one 5" square of Cream Belfast Linen (32 ct), embroidery floss (see color key), and one 3¾"h x 4" dia. crystal jar (2⅝" dia. lid opening).

1. Follow **Working On Linen**, page 156, to work design over 2 fabric threads, using 2 strands of floss for Cross Stitch and 1 for Backstitch.
2. Insert stitched piece in jar lid.

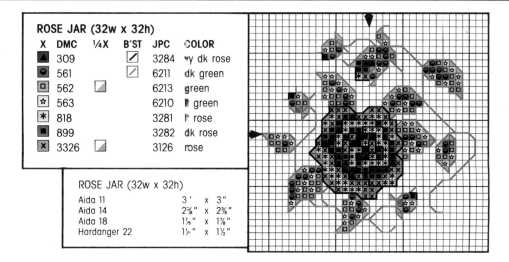

ROSE JAR (32w x 32h)

X	DMC	¼X	B'ST	JPC	COLOR
▲	309		╱	3284	vy dk rose
◕	561		╱	6211	dk green
▣	562	◨		6213	green
☆	563			6210	lt green
✳	818			3281	lt rose
■	899			3282	dk rose
✕	3326	◨		3126	rose

ROSE JAR (32w x 32h)

Aida 11	3"	x 3"
Aida 14	2⅜"	x 2⅜"
Aida 18	1⅞"	x 1⅞"
Hardanger 22	1½"	x 1½"

GRANNY SQUARE AFGHAN (Shown on page 29)

The afghan we used as a tree skirt is an antique. These instructions have been developed to enable you to make a reproduction. Due to the progress made in the manufacture of yarn and the change in consumer demands, it may not be possible to find colors exactly like those in our afghan. However, there is a wide variety of suitable yarn available, and you should be able to create an heirloom that is just as beautiful!

Finished Size: approximately 48" x 72"

ABBREVIATIONS

CC	Contrasting Color
ch(s)	chain(s)
dc	double crochet(s)
MC	Main Color
Rnd	Round(s)
sc	single crochet
sp(s)	space(s)

† or ★ — work instructions following † or ★ as many **more** times as indicated in addition to the first time.

( ) — work enclosed instructions **as many** times as specified by the number immediately following **or** contains explanatory remarks.

MATERIALS

3-ply Fingering Yarn, approximately:
   MC (Black) — 15 ounces, (425 grams, 2600 yards)
   Color A (Ecru) — ½ ounce, (15 grams, 80 yards)
   Color B (Pink) — ¾ ounce, (20 grams, 125 yards)
   Color C (Purple) — 3 ounces, (90 grams, 540 yards)
   CC (Scraps) — 15½ ounces, (435 grams, 2655 yards)
Steel crochet hook, size 1 (2.75 mm) **or** size needed for gauge
Yarn needle

GAUGE: One square = 2¼"
   DO NOT HESITATE TO CHANGE HOOK SIZE TO OBTAIN CORRECT GAUGE.

BORDER SQUARE (Make 64)

With Color A, ch 4, join with slip st to form a ring.
Rnd 1 (Right side): Ch 3 (counts as first dc, now and throughout), 2 dc in ring, ch 2 (3 dc in ring, ch 2) 3 times; join with slip st to first dc, finish off: 4 ch-2 sps.

Note: Loop a short piece of yarn around any stitch to mark last round as **right side**.

Rnd 2: With right side facing, join Color B with sc in any ch-2 sp; ch 3, (2 dc, ch 2, 3 dc) in same sp, ch 1, ★ (3 dc, ch 2, 3 dc) in next ch-2 sp, ch 1; repeat from ★ 2 more times; join with slip st to first dc, finish off.

Rnd 3: With right side facing, join Color C with sc in any ch-2 sp; ch 3, (2 dc, ch 2, 3 dc) in same sp, ch 1, 3 dc in next ch-1 sp, ch 1, ★ (3 dc, ch 2, 3 dc) in next ch-2 sp, ch 1, 3 dc in next ch-1 sp, ch 1; repeat from ★ 2 more times; join with slip st to first dc, finish off.

Rnd 4: With right side facing, join MC with sc in any ch-2 sp; ch 3, (2 dc, ch 2, 3 dc) in same sp, (ch 1, 3 dc in next ch-1 sp) twice; ★ ch 1, (3 dc, ch 2, 3 dc) in next ch-2 sp, (ch 1, 3 dc in next ch-1 sp) twice; repeat from ★ 2 more times; join with slip st to first dc, finish off.

INSIDE SQUARE (Make 463)

Follow Border Square instructions, substituting CC for Colors A, B, and C.

JOINING

Refer to Diagram to join squares. With wrong sides of 2 squares together and using MC, whipstitch squares together (**Fig. 1**) beginning at any ch-2 space on both squares and ending at next ch-2 space.

Fig. 1

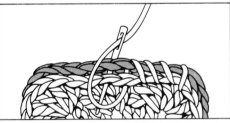

EDGING

Rnd 1: With right side of afghan facing, join Color C with sl st in ch-2 sp where indicated by Point A on Diagram; ch 3, (2 dc, ch 2, 3 dc) in same sp, † ★ (ch 1, 3 dc in next ch-1 sp) 3 times, ch 1, dc in inside corner (Point B), ch 1, (3 dc in next ch-1 sp, ch 1) 3 times, (3 dc, ch 2, 3 dc) in next ch-2 sp; repeat from ★ to corner of afghan (Point C); (ch 1, 3 dc in next ch-1 sp) 3 times, ch 1, (3 dc, ch 2, 3 dc) in next

ch-2 sp; repeat from † around; join with sl st to first st, finish off.

Rnd 2: With right side facing and beginning at Point A on Diagram, join MC with sc in ch-2 sp in Row 1 of edging; ch 4, sl st in fourth ch from hook, sc in same ch-1 sp, † ★ (skip next dc, sc in next 2 dc, sc in next ch-1 sp, ch 4, sl st in fourth ch from hook, sc in same ch-1 sp) 3 times, skip next dc, sc in next 2 dc, sc in next 2 ch-1 sps, skip next dc, sc in next 2 dc (sc in next ch-1 sp, ch 4, sl st in fourth ch from hook, sc in same ch-1 sp, skip next dc, sc in next 2 dc) 3 times, sc in next ch-2 sp, ch 4, sl st in fourth ch from hook, sc in same ch-2 sp. Repeat from ★ to corner. (Skip next dc, sc in next 2 dc, sc in next ch-1 sp, ch 4, sl st in fourth ch from hook, sc in same ch-1 sp) 4 times, skip next dc, sc in next 2 dc, sc in next ch-1 sp, ch 4, sl st in fourth ch from hook, sc in same ch-1 sp. Repeat from † around; join with sl st to first st, finish off.

DIAGRAM

■ border square
□ inside square

FLORAL CONE ORNAMENTS (Shown on page 31)

For each ornament, you will need 1 handkerchief (one 10½" square handkerchief will make 4 ornaments; we found our handkerchiefs at local antique stores and flea markets), two 8" squares of fabric, 10" of ½"w flat lace trim, three 20" lengths of desired width satin ribbon in coordinating colors, tracing paper, thread to match fabric, polyester fiberfill, and dried white baby's breath.

1. Trace cone pattern on this page onto tracing paper and cut out. Use pattern and cut 2 cone pieces from fabric squares.
2. Place 1 cone piece (front) right side up on a flat surface. Referring to **Fig. 1**, place 1 corner of handkerchief right side up on fabric piece with corner of handkerchief 1⅜" from each straight edge of fabric piece; pin in place. Trim handkerchief even with curved edge of

fabric piece; reserve remainder of handkerchief for other cones.

Fig. 1

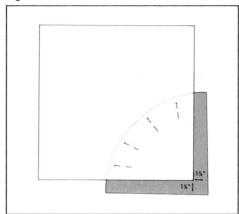

3. With right sides together, match straight edge of lace trim and curved edge of cone front; baste lace trim to right side of cone piece over

handkerchief.
4. Matching right sides and raw edges, place remaining cone piece on top of handkerchief and front cone piece. Use a ¼" seam allowance and sew fabric pieces together along curved edge. Clip seam allowance and turn cone right side out; press.
5. Matching right sides (handkerchief side) and straight edges, fold cone in half. Use a ¼" seam allowance and sew straight edges together. Trim seam allowance and turn cone right side out.
6. Knot ribbon lengths together 3" from each end. With seam of cone at center back, refer to photo and tack 1 ribbon knot to cone ½" from top edge on each side.
7. Lightly stuff bottom half of cone with fiberfill. Fill remainder of cone with baby's breath.

CONE

You will need one 24" x 18" piece of fabric for stocking, one 24" x 18" piece of fabric for lining, one 1½" x 5" piece of fabric for hanger, one approx. 10" square handkerchief for cuff (we found our crochet-edged handkerchief at a local antique store), thread to match fabrics, and tracing paper.

1. Matching registration marks (⊕) and overlapping pattern pieces, trace stocking pattern, page 37, onto tracing paper and cut out.
2. For stocking, use pattern and cut 2 pieces from fabric, 1 in reverse. With right sides together and leaving top edge open, use a ¼" seam allowance and sew pieces together. Clip seam allowance and turn right side out; press.
3. For cuff, use cuff pattern on this page and follow **Transferring Patterns**, page 156. Referring to **Fig. 1** for pattern placement, use pattern and cut 1 cuff from handkerchief.

Fig. 1

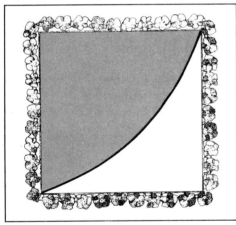

4. Referring to photo, match raw edges and place wrong side of cuff on right side of stocking. Use a ¼" seam allowance and sew cuff to stocking, easing cuff as necessary. Press top edge of stocking ½" to wrong side.
5. For lining, use lining fabric and repeat Step 2; do not turn right side out. Press top edge ½" to wrong side.
6. With wrong sides together, insert lining into stocking and pin in place.
7. For hanger, press long edges of fabric piece ¼" to wrong side. With wrong sides together, fold hanger piece in half lengthwise; press. Sew long edges together. Matching ends, fold hanger in half to form a loop. Place ends of hanger between lining and stocking at heel side with approximately

1½" of loop extending above stocking; pin in place.
8. Slipstitch lining to stocking and, at the same time, securely sew hanger in place.

CUFF

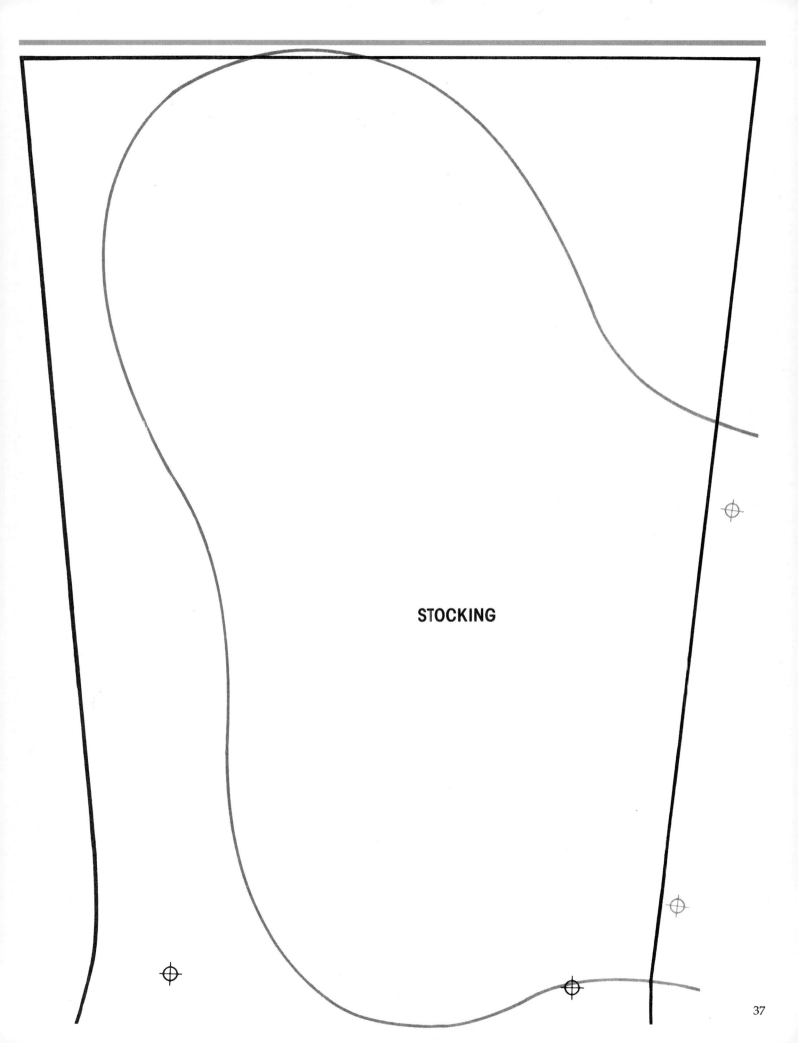

STOCKING

A FESTIVAL OF TREES

Part of the joy of Christmas comes from decorating our homes for the holidays. Along with setting up a traditional tree in the living room, many of us delight in spreading cheer to every corner of the house. This festival of small trees celebrates many moods — from turn-of-the-century nostalgia to childlike excitement — so there's something to please everyone! Instructions for the projects shown here and on the next four pages begin on page 44.

This **Old-fashioned Santa Tree** (*page 47*) features a collection of papier mâché ornaments. Hand-shaped and painted, each Santa has a unique personality.

Reminiscent of yesteryear, the elegant **Postcard Tree** *(page 50)* displays your treasured holiday postcards, whether antiques or reproductions. Touches of gold highlight traditional crackers and bargello ornaments, while tiny white lights and a jeweled garland add sparkle.

With Christmas messages from children tied to its branches, this colorful **Letters to Santa Tree** *(page 45)* is a fun way to enjoy the season. The heart-shaped **Santa Pillow** *(page 46)* makes a whimsical accent.

Placed near the front door, the **Christmas Wish Tree** *(page 48)* is a nice way to share hopes for the holidays and the coming year. Visitors will enjoy choosing the bunny, bear, or cat expressing their favorite wish to take with them when they leave. A basket of extra ornaments can be kept nearby to replenish the tree.

The snowy branches of the **Holiday Cardinal Tree** *(page 45)* are inhabited by a colorful flock of birds.
A garland of grapevine and an assortment of natural items create a fresh, woodsy look.

This decorative **Feathered Friends' Cottage**
(page 44) is a charming addition to a table.
Surrounded by a picket fence, the **Partridge in
a Pear Tree** *(page 44)* features handcrafted pear
ornaments and a plump little partridge.

PARTRIDGE IN A PEAR TREE (Shown on page 43)

Happily roosting among golden Pears made from modeling compound, a charming artificial partridge counts the days of Christmas. The Twig Tree and Bag are easy to make and bring the country indoors. The scene is complete when the tree is enclosed with a cheerful Picket Fence created from painted craft sticks and household screen.

TWIG TREE AND BAG

For tree, you will need one 6" dia. clay flowerpot, plaster of paris, several twiggy branches with leaves, a 3" high artificial partridge, florist wire, hot glue gun and glue sticks (optional), and masking tape.

For bag, you will need one 16" x 31" piece of burlap, thread to match burlap, 1 yd of 3-ply jute, a large needle, and polyester fiberfill.

1. For tree, use tape to cover drain hole in flowerpot.
2. Follow manufacturer's instructions to mix enough plaster of paris to fill flowerpot to 1" from top. Pour plaster into flowerpot and insert branches into plaster, arranging as desired. If necessary, prop branches in place until plaster is dry.
3. For bag, match short edges and fold burlap in half (folded edge is 1 side edge). Using a ½" seam allowance, sew along bottom edge and remaining side edge. Turn bag right side out. Beginning at 1 side of bag, use jute and a long Running Stitch, page 156, to stitch 2½" from top of bag. Fringe top of bag 1".
4. Place flowerpot in bag and stuff fiberfill into bag around pot. Knot each end of jute; tie jute into a bow.
5. Wire partridge to tree. Use glue to secure any loose leaves.

PEARS

For each yellow pear, you will need yellow Sculpey III Modeling Compound and Primrose Folk Art® acrylic paint.
For each lt brown pear, you will need translucent Sculpey III Modeling Compound and Strawberry Parfait Folk Art® acrylic paint.
You will also need 24-gauge gold wire, whole cloves, and Design Master® glossy wood tone spray (available at craft stores).

1. Follow manufacturer's instructions to soften modeling compound. For pear shape, form 1 approximately 1" dia. ball and 1 approximately ½" dia. ball from modeling compound. Press large ball lightly on a flat surface to flatten 1 side (bottom). Referring to photo, press small ball onto top of large ball and smooth balls together.
2. For stem, press bud end of clove into top of pear shape.
3. For hanger, bend a 2" length of wire in half to form a loop. Leaving ¼" of loop exposed, insert ends of wire into top of pear next to stem.
4. Follow manufacturer's instructions to harden modeling compound.
5. Referring to photo, use index finger to dab paint on 1 side of pear; allow to dry.
6. Concentrating more spray on painted area of pear, lightly spray entire pear with wood tone spray. Allow to dry.

PICKET FENCE

You will need ¾" x 6" craft sticks, aluminum screen wire, utility scissors, red acrylic paint, Design Master® glossy wood tone spray (available at craft stores), Aleene's Thick Designer Tacky Glue®, foam brush, plastic wrap, and heavy books.

1. Referring to photo, use utility scissors to cut a point at 1 end of each craft stick. Trim remaining end of each stick straight across so that stick measures 5" long.
2. Paint sticks; allow to dry. Lightly spray with wood tone spray; allow to dry.
3. For each 10½" fence section, cut two ½" x 11¼" strips of screen wire. Referring to **Fig. 1**, place 7 sticks on a flat surface with straight ends even; glue wire strips to sticks. Cover fence with plastic wrap and weight with books until glue dries. Repeat for remaining fence sections.

Fig. 1

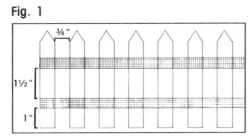

4. To assemble fence, remove plastic wrap from fence sections. Overlapping ends ¾", glue wire strip ends of 1 fence section to wire strip ends on first stick of next section. Repeat with remaining sections to form a loop.

FEATHERED FRIENDS' COTTAGE

(Shown on page 43)

You will need desired birdhouse (we found our 5½" x 7" x 10" birdhouse at a local garden center); Design Master® glossy wood tone spray (available at craft stores); small pieces of cellulose sponge; hot glue gun; glue sticks; dk green, green, lt green, red, and cream acrylic paints; ¾" x 6" craft sticks; utility scissors; tracing paper; 36-gauge copper tooling foil (available at craft stores); brown paint pen with a fine point; fine steel wool; matte clear acrylic spray; ruler; screwdriver; wire cake rack; ½" tacks; and hammer.

1. If desired, spray house evenly with wood tone spray; allow to dry.
2. For greenery, dampen sponge pieces and squeeze out excess water. Referring to photo, use a sponge piece and an up-and-down stamping motion to apply a light coat of paint to front and sides of house in the following order: dk green, green, and lt green. Allow to dry.
3. Referring to photo and cutting sticks desired lengths, follow Steps 1 and 2 of Picket Fence instructions on this page. Glue sticks to front of house.
4. (**Note:** Cut edges of tooling foil may be sharp.) Trace sign pattern onto tracing paper and cut out. Use pattern and cut 1 sign from tooling foil.
5. Paint sign cream; allow to dry. Referring to photo, use paint pen to print "WELCOME"; allow to dry. Lightly spray sign with wood tone spray. Rub edges of sign lightly with steel wool. Glue sign above opening of house.
6. Apply 1 coat of acrylic spray to house; allow to dry.
7. Measure length and width of roof of house and add 1" to each measurement. Cut tooling foil the determined measurements.
8. Measuring ¼" from 1 edge of foil, use ruler and screwdriver to score a fold line. Repeat for remaining edges.
9. Place ruler against 1 score line; bend foil over ruler. Repeat to bend remaining edges to 1 side (wrong side).
10. For roof indentations, place foil right side up on cake rack. Pressing firmly, rub handle of screwdriver over foil to create raised lines.
11. Refer to photo to tack foil to roof.

HOLIDAY CARDINAL TREE (Shown on page 42)

An artificial tree only 4 feet tall is big on holiday spirit when filled with festive red cardinals and an assortment of natural elements. Everything on this tree can be found at home or at a local florist or craft store, making it quick to decorate.

Placed in a dark brown woven basket, the base of this tree is concealed by a snowy layer of cotton quilt batting. Cotton batting is also torn into pieces and used as snow to decorate the branches. Once the snowy scene has been set, other decorations are added.

Green eucalyptus, sweet gum balls, and assorted dried pods are spritzed lightly with gold spray paint. Placed among the branches, these items add a shimmery glow. Pinecones of different sizes add texture, and a garland of grapevine encircling the tree is the perfect place for artificial cardinals to perch. The 1½" and 4" high cardinals are also wired to tree branches.

Sprays of artificial holly and red berries provide additional red accents, while sprigs of dried white ti-tree add airy touches of white. For a final festive touch, bows made from ⅞" wide plaid ribbon are wired in place, and drifts of artificial snow are sprinkled over the tree.

LETTERS TO SANTA TREE (Shown on page 40)

Our 4-foot-tall tree will evoke warm childhood memories of those letters written to Santa Claus in a childlike scrawl. The tree is trimmed with a wooden bead garland in primary colors and sprinkled with 2½" diameter jingle bells, Mitten Ornaments, and Letters to Santa. Jumbo crayons are added to the tree by hot gluing a short length of florist wire to one side of each crayon and twisting the wire around a branch. Underneath the tree, a cozy plaid stadium blanket adds warmth and charm.

MITTEN ORNAMENTS

For each ornament, you will need four 5½" squares of fabric for mittens, two 1" x 5" strips of artificial lamb fleece for cuffs, thread to match fabric and fleece, small crochet hook to turn fabric, 7" of yarn, fabric marking pencil, and tracing paper.

1. Use mitten pattern and follow **Transferring Patterns** and **Sewing Shapes**, page 156, to make 2 mittens from fabric squares. Do not turn right side out.
2. For cuff, match right sides and short edges and fold 1 fleece strip in half. Using a ¼" seam allowance, sew short edges together to form a loop. Repeat for remaining fleece strip.
3. With right side of cuff and wrong side of mitten facing, match 1 long raw edge of 1 cuff to raw edge of mitten. Using a ¼" seam allowance, sew raw edges together. Turn mitten right side out and fold cuff down over mitten. Repeat for remaining mitten.
4. Place 1 end of yarn inside 1 mitten at thumb side; securely tack in place. Repeat to attach remaining end of yarn to remaining mitten.

LETTERS TO SANTA

For each letter, you will need one 3½" x 5" piece of manuscript paper (available at school supply stores); one 3½" x 5" piece of lightweight cardboard; spray adhesive; hole punch; red colored pencil; and 20" lengths of desired widths of red, yellow, and blue satin ribbon.

1. Referring to photo, use pencil to write letter on paper.
2. Matching edges, use spray adhesive to secure letter to cardboard.
3. Referring to photo, punch a hole in upper left corner of letter. Thread ribbons through hole; use ribbons to tie letter to tree.

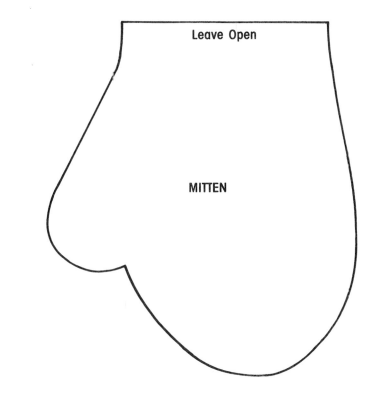

Leave Open

MITTEN

Continued on page 46

TREETOP HAT

You will need one 18" square of fabric for hat, one 6" x 22½" piece of artificial lamb fleece for trim, thread to match fabric and fleece, one 1¼" dia. jingle bell, fabric marking pencil, string, thumbtack or pin, and small crochet hook (to turn fabric).

1. For hat, tie 1 end of string to fabric marking pencil. Insert thumbtack through string 17" from pencil. Insert thumbtack in 1 corner of fabric as shown in **Fig. 1** and mark cutting line; cut out.

Fig. 1

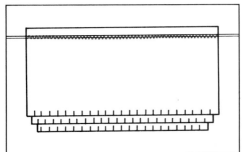

2. With right sides facing and matching straight edges, fold hat piece in half. Using a ½" seam allowance, sew straight edges together. Cut corner diagonally and turn right side out. Use the rounded end of crochet hook to completely turn hat point.

3. For trim, match right sides and short edges and fold fleece in half; using a ½" seam allowance, sew short edges together to form a loop. Press seam open.

4. With wrong sides together, match raw edges and fold trim in half. Baste raw edges together.

5. Baste ½" and ¼" from raw edge of hat. Pull basting threads, drawing up gathers to fit trim. Matching seams and raw edges, baste trim to wrong side of hat.

6. Using a ½" seam allowance, sew trim to hat. Fold up trim on hat and tack in place.

7. Sew jingle bell to point of hat.

SANTA PILLOW   (Shown on page 40)

You will need two 17" squares of unbleached muslin fabric for pillow, three 8" x 12" pieces of unbleached muslin fabric for beard, one 10" square of fabric for hat, one 1" x 12" piece of artificial lamb fleece for hat trim, 3-ply jute, one 1" dia. red shank button for nose, two ³⁄₁₆" dia. black buttons for eyes, one ¾" dia. jingle bell, powder blush, instant coffee, tracing paper, fabric marking pencil, polyester fiberfill, string, thumbtack or pin, transparent tape, hot glue gun, and glue sticks.

1. Dissolve 1 tablespoon of instant coffee in 1 cup of hot water; allow to cool. Soak muslin pieces in coffee for several minutes. Remove from coffee and allow to dry; press.

2. For pillow pattern, use pillow top and bottom patterns on this page and follow **Transferring Patterns**, page 156. Matching registration marks (⊕), overlap top and bottom patterns to form complete pattern; tape patterns together.

3. For pillow, follow **Sewing Shapes**, page 156. Stuff pillow with fiberfill; sew final closure by hand.

4. For beard, match edges and stack 8" x 12" muslin pieces together. Cut a 1 yd length of jute. Leaving 12" of jute at each end of beard, place jute ½" from 1 long edge of stack. Using a medium width zigzag stitch with a medium stitch length, sew jute to muslin pieces. Trim seam allowance close to stitching.

5. At approximately ½" intervals, clip ¼" into long edges of each fabric piece, staggering clips as shown in **Fig. 1**. At each clip, tear fabric up to zigzag-stitched line.

Fig. 1

6. Cut two 20" lengths of jute. Referring to photo, tie each length into a bow; tack 1 bow to each side of beard.

7. For hat, follow Steps 1 and 2 of Treetop Hat instructions on this page, inserting thumbtack through string 9" from pencil. For trim, glue fleece strip along bottom edge of hat. Sew jingle bell to point of hat.

8. Referring to photo, place hat over point of pillow and glue in place. Tie beard around pillow; glue top edge of beard in place. Sew buttons for nose and eyes to pillow. Apply blush to cheeks.

PILLOW TOP

PILLOW BOTTOM

A small feather tree is the perfect setting for these unique Santa ornaments. Shaped by hand from papier mâché over a foil base and painted in different ways, each Santa has his own personality. A simple red bead garland strung among the branches complements these expressive gentlemen.

PAPIER MÂCHÉ SANTA ORNAMENTS

For each ornament, you will need 1 approx. 2" long bobby pin, aluminum foil, instant papier mâché (we used Celluclay® Instant Papier Mâché; a 1 lb. package will make approx. 30 ornaments), resealable plastic bag (optional), toothpicks, gesso, acrylic paint (see Step 2 of Painting and Decorating Santa instructions, page 48, for colors), small round paintbrushes, dk brown waterbase stain, foam brush, a soft cloth, glitter and craft glue (optional), and matte clear acrylic spray.

Note: Refer to photo when shaping, painting, and decorating ornaments. Use measurements given in instructions as general guidelines; variations in the Santas add to their handmade charm.

SHAPING HOODED SANTA

1. Separate prongs of bobby pin slightly (**Fig. 1**).

Fig. 1

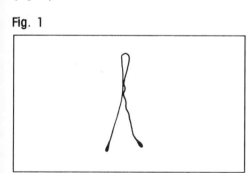

2. Leaving top ¼" of bobby pin exposed for hanger, wrap and crush a 12" square of foil firmly between and around prongs, forming a rounded oblong shape. Wrap additional pieces of foil around shape as needed to fill out head shape. Foil head should be well shaped and firm before papier mâché is added (**Fig. 2**).

Fig. 2.

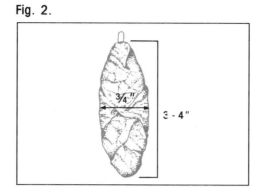

3. Following manufacturer's instructions, mix papier mâché with water. (Excess mixture can be stored in a plastic bag in refrigerator for up to 4 days.)
4. Apply an approximately ⅛" thick layer of papier mâché over foil, smoothing papier mâché with fingers.
5. Refer to **Fig. 3** and use the wooden end of a paintbrush to make a small round hole in papier mâché for mouth. Use a toothpick to press lines into papier mâché for face and beard as shown in **Fig. 3**. For nose, add a small piece of papier mâché to face, smoothing edges. Hang ornament to dry.

Fig. 3

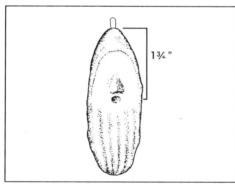

6. Follow Painting and Decorating Santa instructions, page 48, to complete ornament.

SHAPING SANTA WITH PLAIN HAT

1. Follow Steps 1 — 4 of Hooded Santa instructions to make Santa head.
2. For hat, form a roll of papier mâché approximately 3½" long and ¼" thick. Refer to **Fig. 4** and wrap roll around head; use fingers to smooth roll onto head and form a pointed ridge for edge of hat. For mouth, use the wooden end of a paintbrush to make a small round hole in papier mâché. For nose, add a small piece of papier mâché to face, smoothing edges. Use a toothpick to press lines into papier mâché to

resemble hair and beard as shown in **Fig. 4**. Hang ornament to dry.

Fig. 4

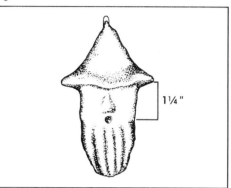

3. Follow Painting and Decorating Santa instructions, page 48, to complete Santa.

SHAPING SANTA WITH FUR-TRIMMED HAT

1. Follow Steps 1 — 4 of Hooded Santa instructions to make Santa head.
2. For fur trim on hat, form a roll of papier mâché approximately 3½" long and ¼" thick. Refer to **Fig. 5** and wrap roll around head. Form a ½" dia. ball of papier mâché; press ball onto top of head over hanging loop, flattening ball on top of head **(Fig. 5)**. Smooth edges of papier mâché onto head to secure. Use a toothpick to press lines in papier mâché to resemble fur. For mouth, use the wooden end of a paintbrush to make a small round hole in papier mâché. For nose, add a small piece of papier mâché to face, smoothing edges. Use a toothpick to press lines into papier mâché to resemble hair and beard as shown in **Fig. 5**. Hang ornament to dry.

Fig. 5

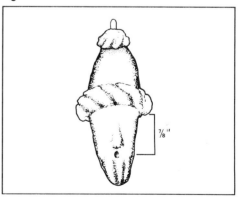

3. Follow Painting and Decorating Santa instructions, page 48, to complete Santa.

Continued on page 48

SANTA TREE (continued)

PAINTING AND DECORATING SANTA
1. Apply 1 coat of gesso to Santa; allow to dry.
2. Paint Santa as follows:
   face — peach or lt pink
   cheeks — dk pink (paint cheeks while face color is still wet, blending cheek color slightly into face color)
   mouth — red
   eyes — white and blue (paint eyes white; add blue dots for pupils)
   beard, hair, eyebrows, and mustache — white, ivory, gold, or brown
   fur trim — white or ivory
   hood or hat — desired color
   decorative motifs (holly, trees, or curlicues) — desired colors
Allow to dry.
3. Apply stain to Santa and remove excess with soft cloth; allow to dry.
4. Spray Santa with acrylic spray; allow to dry.
5. To add glitter to Santa, apply glue where desired. Sprinkle glitter over glue, coating well. Allow to dry. Shake off excess glitter.

CHRISTMAS WISH TREE (Shown on page 41)

Those things that we wish for others at Christmastime are written on the simple pinafores of our Christmas Wish Ornaments. These ornaments are displayed on a tabletop tree along with purchased butter cookies tied on with ⅜" wide red satin ribbon.

CHRISTMAS WISH ORNAMENTS
For each ornament, you will need 1 approx. 5" x 8" foam meat tray (available in meat department of grocery store), foam brushes, gesso, craft knife, tracing paper, graphite transfer paper, acrylic paint (see color key, on this page or page 49, for colors), small round paintbrush, #00 liner paintbrush, fabric glue, 1" square pieces of cellulose sponge, removable fabric marking pen, one 8" x 15" piece of fabric for dress, one 8½" x 13" piece of unbleached muslin fabric for pinafore, instant coffee, thread to match fabrics, black permanent felt-tip pen with fine point, and coordinating embroidery floss.

1. Trace cat, bear, or rabbit pattern, on this page or page 49, onto tracing paper.
2. Use transfer paper and a dull pencil to transfer pattern to smooth side of meat tray; use craft knife to cut out.
3. (**Note:** Refer to photo and color key, on this page or page 49, for Steps 3 — 6.) Apply 2 coats of gesso, then 2 coats of basecoat to entire ornament, allowing to dry between coats.
4. For rabbit or bear, dampen a sponge piece and squeeze out excess water. Use sponge piece and an up-and-down stamping motion to paint ornament with grey or brown paint, allowing some of basecoat to show through. For bear, repeat with another sponge piece and dk brown paint. Allow to dry.
5. For cat, trace stripe pattern, page 49, onto tracing paper and cut out. Use pattern and cut 2 stripe shapes from sponge. Dampen sponge pieces and squeeze out excess water. Use 1 sponge shape and brown paint to stamp stripes on ornament; use remaining sponge

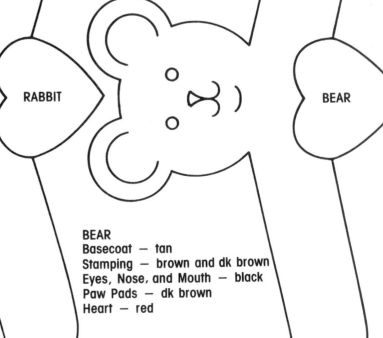

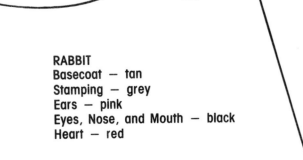

RABBIT
Basecoat — tan
Stamping — grey
Ears — pink
Eyes, Nose, and Mouth — black
Heart — red

BEAR
Basecoat — tan
Stamping — brown and dk brown
Eyes, Nose, and Mouth — black
Paw Pads — dk brown
Heart — red

shape and white paint to stamp additional stripes on ornament. Allow to dry.

6. Paint facial features and heart. Allow to dry.

7. For dress, use dress pattern and follow **Transferring Patterns**, page 156.

8. Matching right sides and short edges, fold dress fabric in half. Placing dress pattern on fold as indicated on pattern, cut out dress.

9. Leaving openings at sleeves and bottom, use a ¼" seam allowance to sew side seams. Clip curves and turn right side out; press.

10. For opening in center back of dress, cut dress open from bottom edge to neck edge.

11. Press raw edges at bottom, sleeve, and back openings ⅛" to wrong side; use fabric glue to secure.

12. Press neck edge ¼" to wrong side, clipping curve as necessary. Baste close to folded edge. Place dress on ornament and pull basting thread to gather fabric to fit around neck; knot threads and trim ends. Tack dress together at back.

13. For pinafore, dissolve 1 tablespoon of instant coffee in 1 cup of hot water; allow to cool. Soak muslin in coffee for several minutes. Remove from coffee and allow to dry; press.

14. Tear a 3¼" square for yoke and two 4" x 6¼" pieces for skirt from muslin.

15. Trace yoke pattern on this page onto tracing paper and cut out. Place pattern on muslin square and use fabric marking pen to draw around neck opening. Cut out opening along pen line.

16. Baste ¼" and ⅛" from 1 long edge of 1 skirt piece. Pull basting threads to gather skirt piece to fit 1 edge of yoke. Overlapping edge of yoke piece and skirt piece ¼", pin yoke to skirt (**Fig. 1**). Repeat to pin remaining skirt piece to opposite edge of yoke (**Fig. 1**).

YOKE

Fig. 1

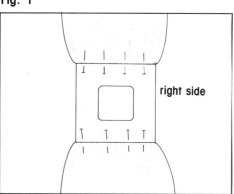

right side

17. Using 2 strands of floss and stitching through all layers, use a Running Stitch, page 156, to sew ⅛" from outside edge and neck opening of yoke.

18. Use black pen to write message on pinafore ½" from bottom edge. With message facing front, place pinafore over dress; tack pinafore skirt together under arms.

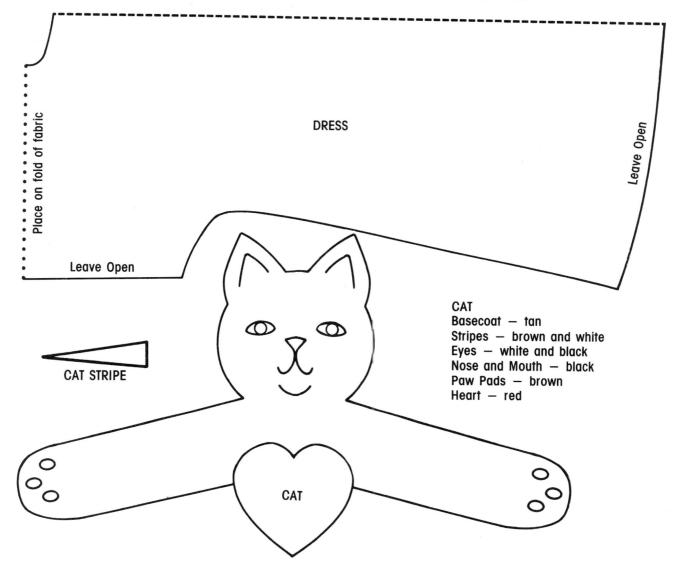

Place on fold of fabric

DRESS

Leave Open

Leave Open

CAT STRIPE

CAT

CAT
Basecoat — tan
Stripes — brown and white
Eyes — white and black
Nose and Mouth — black
Paw Pads — brown
Heart — red

POSTCARD TREE (Shown on page 39)

Sending best wishes for the season, this live 5-foot-tall Canadian hemlock is placed in a large bucket which has been covered with lush red fabric and tied with exquisite French ribbon. The delicate branches are decked with sparkling white lights and purchased jeweled garland. Carefully placed antique or reproduction postcards make unusual, attractive ornaments. Elegant Plastic Canvas Ornaments and Crackers glitter among the branches to complete this Christmas treasure.

PLASTIC CANVAS ORNAMENTS

For Ornament #1, you will need 10 mesh plastic canvas (one 10½" x 13½" sheet will make 3 ornaments), one 3" dia. plastic canvas circle, Balger® metallic gold ⅛"w ribbon (8 yds), and the following colors of embroidery floss: 6 skeins of cream (DMC 739), 9 skeins of red (DMC 498), and 9 skeins of green (DMC 890).

For Ornament #2, you will need 10 mesh plastic canvas (one 10½" x 13½" sheet will make 6 ornaments), Balger® metallic gold ⅛"w ribbon (one 5½ yd spool), and the following colors of embroidery floss: 9 skeins of cream (DMC 739), 9 skeins of red (DMC 498), and 9 skeins of green (DMC 890).

For Ornament #3, you will need 10 mesh plastic canvas (one 10½" x 13½" sheet will make 6 ornaments), Balger® metallic gold ⅛"w ribbon (one 5½ yd spool), and the following colors of embroidery floss: 6 skeins of cream (DMC 739) and 15 skeins of red (DMC 498).

1. (**Note:** To cut plastic canvas pieces accurately, count threads, not holes.) Follow charts to cut out plastic canvas pieces.

2. (**Note:** Gobelin Stitch and Overcast Stitch, page 157, are used to stitch ornaments. Use 18 strands of embroidery floss; use 1 strand of metallic ribbon.) Leaving stitches in grey area unworked, follow charts and use required stitches to work Ornament and Ornament Top (for Ornament #1 or #3 only).

3. To join ends of ornament, match ●'s and ■'s and overlap stitched end over unstitched flap; work stitches in grey area through 2 thicknesses to join ends.

4. (**Note:** To join remaining edges, use green for Ornament #1, gold for Ornament #2, and red for Ornament

#3.) Referring to photo and working from each ■ or ✳ to bottom point, join edges of bottom of ornament; working from each ● or □ to top of ornament, join edges of top of ornament.

5. For Ornament #1 or #3, thread 8" of gold up through Ornament Top at 1 **x**

and down through Top at remaining **x**; knot ends together on back of Top. Join Top to Ornament. For Ornament #2, thread 8" of gold through top of ornament at **x**'s. Knot ends together and conceal knot in top point of ornament.

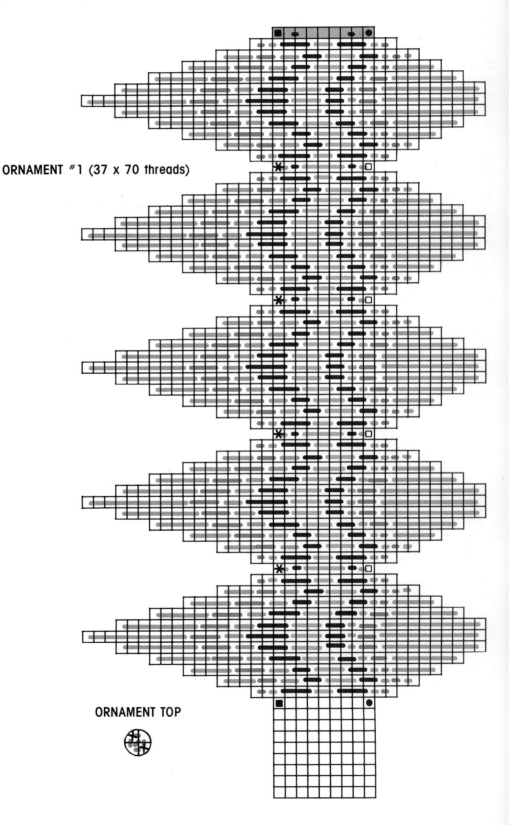

ORNAMENT #1 (37 x 70 threads)

ORNAMENT TOP

ORNAMENT #2 (39 x 42 threads)

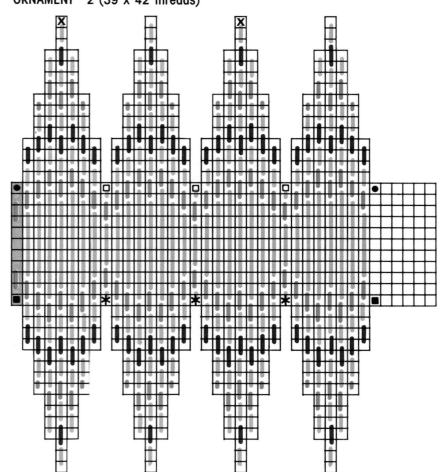

CRACKERS

For each cracker, you will need 25" of ⅛"w gold braid, 5¾" of 1½"w craft ribbon, one 8" x 12" piece of crepe paper, one 3" x 5" index card, transparent tape, and double-sided transparent tape.

1. Overlapping short edges ¼", roll index card into a tube; use transparent tape to secure.
2. Center tube on 1 short edge of crepe paper. Roll paper around tube; use double-sided tape to secure overlapped edge.
3. Cut gold braid in half. Refer to photo to tie 1 length of braid in a bow around each end of rolled paper close to tube.
4. Refer to photo to wrap ribbon around cracker, overlapping ends; use double-sided tape to secure.

cream
red
green
metallic gold

ORNAMENT #3 (47 x 36 threads)

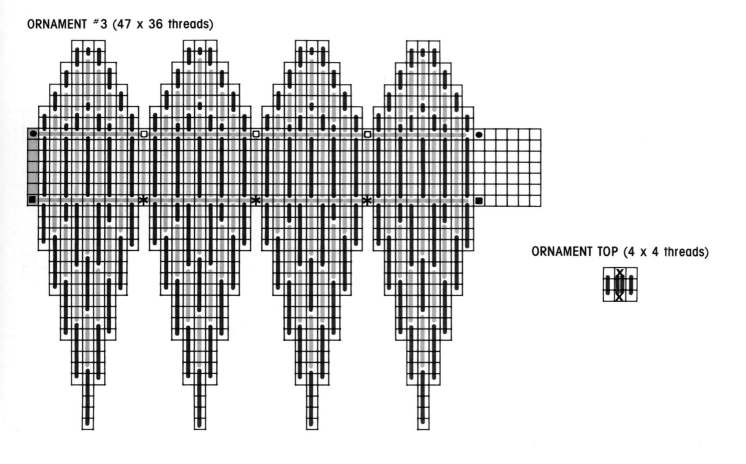

ORNAMENT TOP (4 x 4 threads)

51

I BELIEVE

From the very first day of December, children everywhere start counting down the days to Santa's arrival. On the long-awaited night before Christmas, a carefully prepared snack is placed near the fireplace before the household settles down for the evening. When Santa arrives at last, he'll be delighted to discover the room filled with these colorful images of himself!

The jolly gift-giver's face can be found throughout this collection, from the wreath above the mantel to the gaily trimmed tree. An array of Advent stockings hangs from the mantel, and giant candy canes complemented by a festive tree skirt add cheer to the scene. There's even a small tree "dressed" as Santa himself, complete with boots and a bag of toys.

These exuberant surroundings are perfect for youngsters — and the young at heart — who truly believe in the magic of Christmas.

Instructions for the projects shown here and on the next four pages begin on page 58.

(*Opposite*) Trimmed with a host of jolly **Santa Ornaments** (*page 58*) and **Giant Stuffed Candy Canes** (*page 63*), the "I Believe" **Tree** (*page 58*) could have been created in Santa's very own North Pole workshop. Bright colored lights, red glass ball ornaments, and a garland of shiny gold beads festoon the branches with cheer. Shown on page 52, the **Ruffled Tree Skirt** (*page 59*) features candy stripes, and a pair of the candy canes cross jauntily atop the tree.

The cross-stitched cuff of this candy-striped "I Believe" **Stocking** (*page 61*) proclaims a childlike trust in Santa Claus.

Marching across the mantel, these **Advent Christmas Stockings** (*page 59*) contain a sweet surprise for each day of the season. What a cute way to count down to Christmas!

Santa's sure to approve of presents wrapped in this colorful **Stamped Gift Wrap** *(page 58)*. Favorite cookie cutter shapes can be used to create the stamped motifs.

This jolly wreath will bring smiles to all your holiday guests! To make it, attach the head and mittens from the **Santa Tree** *(page 62)* to an evergreen wreath. A festive **Giant Stuffed Candy Cane** *(page 63)* and a gaily wrapped package complete the arrangement.

(Opposite) This **Santa Tree** *(page 62)* will delight children of all ages! We created this merry fellow on a small scale so the youngsters can relate to him. Your favorite little girl will be a real-life Christmas charmer clad in the adorable "I Believe" Romper *(page 60)*.

"I BELIEVE" TREE

(Shown on page 52)

This 7-foot-tall tree is filled with beaming Santa ornaments that are sure to capture every child's heart — convincing young and old alike to "believe" in the spirit of the holiday season.

Decorations for the tree begin with strings of purchased multicolored lights. Their happy glow lights up the faces of the papier mâché Santa Ornaments (on this page). Even children will want to lend a hand with these ornaments made from balloons, newspaper, and polyester fiberfill. Wrapped with ribbon, Giant Stuffed Candy Canes (page 63) are hung on the branches, and two crisscrossed candy canes are tacked together to provide a jaunty treetop decoration. Purchased gold bead garland adds a sparkling finish. At the base of the tree, an inviting Ruffled Tree Skirt (page 59) awaits the arrival of gifts to be brought by Santa.

STAMPED GIFT WRAP

(Shown on page 56)

You will need large baking potatoes (1 potato will make 2 stamps), desired cookie cutters, foam brushes, red and green acrylic paint, butcher or banner paper, green felt-tip pen with medium point, and paring knife.

1. (**Note:** Follow Steps 1 — 3 for each stamped design.) Cut 1 potato in half lengthwise.
2. Center 1 cookie cutter on cut side of 1 potato half; press cutter ¼" into potato and remove cookie cutter. Leaving cookie cutter design raised ¼" for stamping, use knife to cut away excess potato around design.
3. Apply an even coat of paint to stamp. Reapplying paint as necessary, stamp designs on paper; allow to dry.
4. Refer to photo and use pen to write "I Believe" on paper.

SANTA ORNAMENTS (Shown on page 54)

For each ornament, you will need 1 round balloon; newspaper; craft glue; ½" dia. white pom-pom; polyester fiberfill; gesso; 6" of 18-gauge cloth-covered florist wire; hot glue gun; glue sticks; artificial holly leaves and berries; peach, black, white, and red acrylic paint; powder blush; and paintbrushes.

1. (**Note:** For Steps 1 — 10, use measurements given as general guidelines.) Blow up balloon to the approximate size of a grapefruit; tie off opening.
2. Tear newspaper into approximately ½" x 4" strips.
3. Mix 2 parts craft glue to 1 part water.
4. Dip 1 strip into glue mixture and pull between fingers to remove excess glue. Place strip on balloon and smooth wrinkles. Overlapping edges of strips, repeat until balloon is covered; allow to dry.
5. Apply 1 coat of gesso to balloon; allow to dry.
6. (**Note:** Use hot glue to assemble ornament.) For hat, refer to **Fig. 1** and use a pencil to draw a line around balloon ⅓ of the way down from the top. For face, draw a triangle 3½" wide and 3" high ½" below hat line. For mouth, draw a semicircle on lower portion of triangle. For nose, glue pom-pom to triangle.

Fig. 1

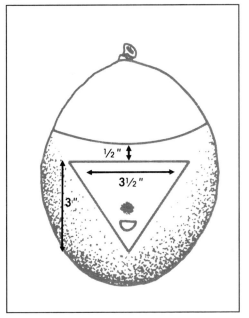

7. For hanger, bend 1 end of wire into a loop. Glue loop to top of balloon.
8. (**Note:** Refer to photo for Steps 8 — 15.) Glue small pieces of fiberfill to front of balloon along face outline. Glue small pieces of fiberfill around balloon, covering hat line. Leaving face and hat uncovered, glue small pieces of fiberfill over remainder of balloon.
9. For mustache, twist an approximately 6" long piece of fiberfill several times in the center. Glue twist under nose, slightly covering top of mouth.
10. For hat top, roll a small piece of fiberfill between hands, forming a 1½" dia. ball. Push wire hanger through center of ball. Glue ball to top of hat, covering wire loop completely.
11. Use paintbrush to apply gesso to fiberfill and nose. Shape beard, mustache, and hat trim with paintbrush and fingers; allow to dry.
12. Paint face and nose peach; allow to dry. Paint hat and mouth red; allow to dry.
13. Refer to **Fig. 2** to paint eyes black; allow to dry. Paint eyebrows white; paint white highlights in eyes. Allow to dry.

Fig. 2

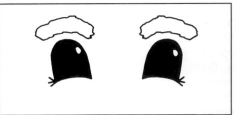

14. Glue leaves and berries to ornament.
15. Apply blush to nose and cheeks.

RUFFLED TREE SKIRT (Shown on page 52)

You will need one 44" square of solid fabric for tree skirt, 2⅛ yds of 44"w striped fabric for ruffle, ½ yd of 44"w solid fabric and 3½ yds of ⅜" dia. cord for cording, thread to match fabrics, yarn or heavy thread, fabric marking pencil, and thumbtack or pin.

1. Fold fabric square in half from top to bottom and again from left to right.
2. To mark outer cutting line, tie 1 end of yarn to fabric marking pencil. Insert thumbtack through yarn 20" from pencil. Insert thumbtack in fabric as shown in **Fig. 1** and mark ¼ of a circle.

Fig. 1

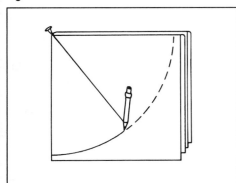

3. To mark inner cutting line, repeat Step 2, inserting thumbtack through yarn 2" from pencil.
4. Cutting through all thicknesses of fabric, cut out skirt along marked lines. For opening in back of skirt, cut along 1 fold from outer to inner edge.

5. Press inner edge of skirt ¼" to wrong side, clipping curve as necessary. Press ¼" to wrong side again; stitch in place. Press each opening edge ¼" to wrong side. Press ¼" to wrong side again; stitch in place.
6. For cording, cut one 2¼"w bias strip 3½ yds long from fabric (pieced as necessary). Press short ends of strip ½" to wrong side. Lay cord along center on wrong side of strip. Matching long edges, fold strip over cord. Use a zipper foot and machine baste along length of strip close to cord. At each end, whipstitch opening closed. With right sides together and matching raw edges, baste cording to skirt.
7. For ruffle, cut a 12"w fabric strip 7⅓ yds long (pieced as necessary). With right sides together, fold strip in half lengthwise. Use a ½" seam allowance and sew along each short edge. Cut corners diagonally; turn right side out. Matching raw edges, press ruffle flat.
8. Place yarn ⅜" from raw edge of ruffle. Leaving 4" of yarn free at each end, use a wide zigzag stitch to stitch over yarn, being careful not to catch yarn in stitching.
9. Pull yarn, gathering ruffle to fit outer edge of skirt; matching right sides and raw edges, pin ruffle to skirt. Use zipper foot and sew ruffle to skirt as close as possible to cording. Press seam allowance toward skirt.

ADVENT CHRISTMAS STOCKINGS

(Shown on page 55)

For each stocking, you will need two 7" x 9" pieces of fabric, 6" of ⅛"w satin ribbon, one 2"w wooden star cutout (available at craft stores), acrylic paint, fabric marking pencil, black paint pen with fine point, thread to match fabric, foam brush, tracing paper, hot glue gun, and glue sticks.

1. Trace stocking pattern on this page onto tracing paper and cut out. Leaving top edge of stocking open, follow **Sewing Shapes**, page 156, to make stocking from fabric pieces.
2. Press top edge of stocking 1" to wrong side.
3. For hanger, fold ribbon in half to form a loop. Place ribbon ends in stocking at heel side with approximately 1½" of loop extending above stocking; tack in place.
4. Paint star; allow to dry. Use pen to paint number on star. Allow to dry. Referring to photo, glue star to stocking.

STOCKING

"I BELIEVE" ROMPER   (Shown on page 57)

Note: Romper is not intended to be used as sleepwear.

You will need 1 men's white crew-neck T-shirt (see Step 1 for size); snap tape (see Step 4 for amount); ½"w elastic; three 1⅝ yd lengths of desired ribbon; white thread; purchased 1"w white bias tape; removable fabric marking pen; cardboard cut to fit snugly inside body of T-shirt; red, yellow, and green fabric paint; ½"w and ¾"w masking tape; 3 small pieces of cellulose sponge; paper towels; 2 large baking potatoes; desired cookie cutters no larger than 2½" x 3½"; paring knife; foam brushes; green squeezable fabric paint pen; and a toothbrush.

1. To determine T-shirt size, measure height of child from shoulder to top of foot; T-shirt should be approximately this long. (We used a men's size large T-shirt to fit a 3-year-old who measured 29" from shoulder to top of foot.) Wash, dry, and press T-shirt.

2. Turn T-shirt wrong side out and lay it back side up on a flat surface. To mark cutting line for inseam, measure inseam of child and subtract 2". Beginning at center bottom edge of T-shirt, use fabric marking pen to draw a line the determined measurement. Cutting through both layers of T-shirt, cut along inseam line. Referring to **Fig. 1**, use a ¼" seam allowance and sew raw edges of inseam together. Turn T-shirt right side out.

Fig. 1

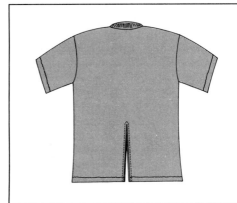

3. Lay T-shirt back side up on a flat surface. To mark cutting line for back opening, begin at top center of neckband and draw a line on T-shirt to within 2½" of inseam. Cutting through back of T-shirt only, cut along back opening line.

4. Measure length of back opening and add ½" to measurement. Cut a length of snap tape determined measurement. Separate snap tape and press ends of each length ½" to wrong side.

5. To attach bottom side of snap tape to right side of opening, press right raw edge of opening ¼" to **right** side. Beginning at top edge of opening, pin snap tape over right raw edge of opening to within ½" of bottom of opening. Sew close to all edges of snap tape to secure (**Fig. 2**). To attach top side of snap tape to left side of opening, press left raw edge of opening ¼" to **wrong** side. Beginning at top edge of opening, pin snap tape over left raw edge (**Fig. 2**); continue pinning snap tape over raw edge to within ½" of bottom of opening. Sew close to all edges of snap tape to secure.

Fig. 2

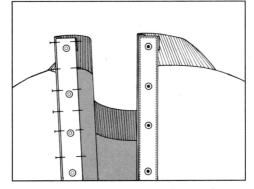

6. To secure bottom ends of snap tape, fasten bottom snap; refer to **Fig. 3** and topstitch a triangle at base of snap tape, stitching over bottom edges of snap tape.

Fig. 3

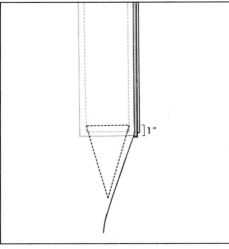

7. (**Note:** Refer to photo for colors and placement of painted design. Practice painting techniques used in Steps 7 – 11 on a scrap piece of fabric before painting romper.) Place cardboard inside romper and fasten snap tape. To paint borders of design on front of romper, refer to **Fig. 4** and use ¾" wide masking tape to mask off horizontal lines on romper (tape shown in light grey); use ½" wide tape to mask off vertical lines on romper (tape shown in dark grey). Dampen 1 sponge piece and squeeze out excess water. Dip sponge into red paint; blot excess on paper towel. Using an up-and-down stamping motion, apply a light coat of red paint to masked off borders as shown in **Fig. 4**. Repeat using green paint for remaining masked off line and yellow paint for small squares. Allow to dry thoroughly. Remove masking tape.

Fig. 4

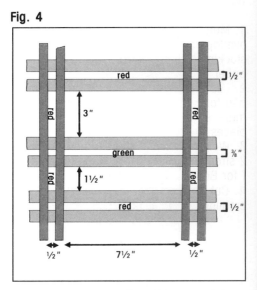

8. Follow Steps 1 – 3 of Stamped Gift Wrap instructions, page 58, to stamp cookie cutter designs on romper.

9. Use paint pen to write "I Believe" on romper. Allow to dry.

10. Cut a 9½" x 4" piece of scrap paper. Cover bottom portion of painted design with paper.

11. To spatter romper, mix 1 part red paint to 1 part water. Dip toothbrush in diluted paint and pull thumb firmly across bristles to spatter paint on romper. Repeat with yellow and green paint. Allow to dry. Remove scrap paper. Repeat to spatter back of romper.

ROMPER (continued)

12. For elastic at sleeves and ankles, measure around 1 sleeve 1" from bottom edge. Cut a length of bias tape 1" longer than determined measurement. Press ends of bias tape ½" to wrong side. Matching wrong sides, pin bias tape to sleeve with 1 long edge of bias tape 1½" from bottom edge of sleeve. Stitching close to each long edge of bias tape, sew tape in place. Measure wrist of child and add 2". Cut a length of elastic determined length. Thread elastic through casing. Overlap ends of elastic 1" and sew ends together. Repeat for remaining sleeve and each ankle.

13. Cut a 14" piece from each length of ribbon; tie pieces together into a bow. Referring to photo, tack bow to 1 sleeve. Repeat for bows on remaining sleeve and ankles.

"I BELIEVE" STOCKING   (Shown on page 55)

You will need two 12" x 20" pieces of fabric for stocking, two 12" x 20" pieces of fabric for lining, one 4¼" x 17" piece of white Aida (14 ct) for cuff, one 4¼" x 17" piece of fabric for cuff lining, lightweight fusible interfacing, one 2¼" x 38" bias strip of fabric (pieced as necessary) and 38" of ¼" dia. cord for cording, one 2" x 5" piece of fabric for hanger, embroidery floss (see color key), thread to match fabrics, tracing paper, and fabric marking pencil.

1. Matching registration marks (⊕) and overlapping pattern pieces, trace stocking pattern, page 37, onto tracing paper and cut out.

2. Leaving top edge open, use pattern and follow **Sewing Shapes**, page 156, to make stocking from stocking fabric pieces. Do not turn right side out.

3. Work "I Believe" design on Aida; use 2 strands of floss for Cross Stitch and 1 for Backstitch.

4. Cut a piece of interfacing slightly smaller than stitched piece. Follow manufacturer's instructions to fuse interfacing to wrong side of stitched piece.

5. For cording, lay cord along center on wrong side of bias strip. Matching long edges, fold strip over cord. Use zipper foot and machine baste along length of strip close to cord. Trim seam allowance to ½" and cut cording in half.

6. For cuff, match right sides and short edges and fold stitched piece in half. Using a ½" seam allowance, sew short ends together to form a tube. Press seam open and turn right side out.

7. Repeat Step 6 with cuff lining fabric. Do not turn cuff lining right side out.

8. Matching right sides and raw edges and starting 1" from end of 1 cording piece, use zipper foot to baste cording to bottom edge of stitched piece. Open ends of cording and cut cord to fit exactly. Insert 1 end of cording fabric in the other; fold raw edge of top fabric ½" to wrong side and baste in place.

9. Place cuff lining and stitched piece right sides together. Using zipper foot and stitching as close as possible to cording, sew lining and stitched piece together along bottom edge. With wrong sides together and matching raw edges, fold cuff in half so that cording shows at lower edge; press.

10. Repeat Step 8 to baste cording to top edge of cuff.

11. Place cuff over stocking with right side of cuff facing wrong side of stocking and matching raw edges. With center of stitched design at center front of stocking, pin cuff in place. Using zipper foot, sew raw edges together close to cording. Turn stocking right side out. Fold cuff down over stocking.

12. For lining, use lining fabric pieces and repeat Step 2. Press top edge of lining ½" to wrong side. With wrong sides facing, insert lining into stocking.

13. For hanger, press long edges of fabric piece ½" to wrong side. With wrong sides together, fold hanger piece in half lengthwise; sew close to folded edges. Fold hanger in half to form a loop. Place ends of hanger between lining and stocking at heel side with approximately 1½" of loop extending above stocking; pin in place.

14. Slipstitch lining to stocking and, at the same time, securely sew hanger in place.

"I BELIEVE" STOCKING (85w x 31h)			
X	DMC	B'ST	JPC	COLOR
■	321		3500	red
◉	726		2294	yellow
	890	◪	6021	dk green
▲	909		6228	green

"I BELIEVE" STOCKING (85w x 31h)	
Aida 11	7¾" x 2⅞"
Aida 14	6⅛" x 2¼"
Aida 18	4¾" x 1¾"
Hardanger 22	3⅞" x 1½"

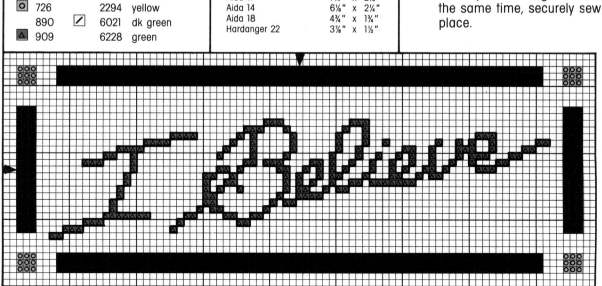

SANTA TREE (Shown on page 57)

For head, you will need two 12" squares of fabric for face, one 4" square of fabric for nose, one 2" x 4" piece of black felt for eyes, white acrylic paint, small flat paintbrush, aerosol hairspray, powder blush, and compass.

For hat and mittens, you will need one 23" x 30" piece of red plush fabric for hat, one 6" x 22" piece of white plush fabric for hat cuff, one 2" dia. white pom-pom, four 9" squares of red plush fabric for mittens, and two 6" x 10¼" pieces of white plush fabric for mitten cuffs.

For belt, you will need 2½ yds of 1¾" wide black vinyl belting, 2" belt buckle kit, and gold metallic spray paint.

For bag, you will need one 45" square of fabric.

You will also need tracing paper, string, fabric marking pen, thumbtack or pin, fabric glue, polyester bonded batting, polyester fiberfill, thread to match fabrics and rope, 1¾ yds of ⅜" dia. hemp rope, red wooden bead garland, red glass ball ornaments in assorted sizes, black boots (we found ours at a military surplus store), florist wire, a 4½-foot-tall artificial Christmas tree, tissue paper, one 36" length of ½" dia. wooden dowel painted green (optional), and assorted toys and candy to fill bag.

1. For face, follow Steps 1 and 2 of Ruffled Tree Skirt instructions, page 59, inserting thumbtack through string 5" from pen. Following cutting line and cutting through all thicknesses of fabric, cut out face piece.

2. Using face piece as a pattern, cut out remaining face fabric square.

3. With right sides facing and leaving an opening for turning, use a ½" seam allowance and sew face fabric pieces together. Clip curves and turn right side out. Stuff firmly with fiberfill; sew final closure by hand.

4. For nose, use compass to draw a 3" dia. circle on wrong side of nose fabric; cut out. Using a double strand of thread, baste ¼" from edge of fabric circle. Pull ends of thread to slightly gather circle. Stuff circle with fiberfill. Folding raw edges to wrong side, pull ends of thread to tightly gather circle; knot thread and trim ends close to knot.

5. For eyes, trace eye pattern onto tracing paper and cut out. Use pattern and cut 2 eyes from felt.

6. Referring to photo, glue eyes at center of face; glue nose below eyes. Paint a small white square for highlight in each eye; allow to dry.

7. Apply blush to cheeks and top of nose.

8. For beard, use beard pattern on this page and follow **Transferring Patterns**, page 156. Use pattern and cut beard from batting. Using a double strand of thread, baste ½" from lower edge of beard. Pull basting threads to slightly gather edge of beard; knot thread at each end and trim ends close to knots.

9. Pulling large flat pieces from fiberfill, glue pieces to 1 side of beard piece (front); allow to dry. Lightly spray beard with hairspray and use fingers to smooth fiberfill.

10. With beard centered 1" below nose, glue top edge of beard to face.

11. For mustache, pull a 6" length from fiberfill. Knot thread around center; trim ends of thread close to knot. Glue center of mustache to face under nose.

12. For hat, cut a 32" square from tracing paper (pieced as necessary). Fold paper in half diagonally and cut apart along fold line. Discard 1 half. Insert thumbtack through string 28½" from pen. Insert thumbtack in corner of paper as shown in **Fig. 1** and mark ⅛ of a circle; cut out. Use pattern and cut 1 hat piece from hat fabric. With right sides together and matching straight edges, fold hat in half. Use a ½" seam allowance to sew straight edges together; clip corner. Do not turn right side out.

BEARD

Fig. 1

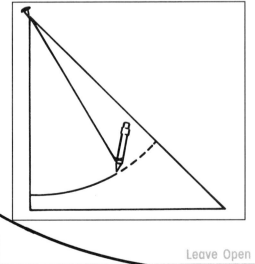

13. For hat cuff, match right sides and short edges of cuff piece and fold in half. Use a ½" seam allowance to sew short edges together to form a tube; finger press seam open. With wrong sides facing and matching raw edges, fold cuff in half. Matching raw edges and seams, place cuff over hat. Use a ½" seam allowance to sew raw edges together. Turn hat right side out and fold cuff to right side. Tack pom-pom to hat point.

14. For mittens, use mitten pattern on this page and follow **Transferring Patterns** and **Sewing Shapes**, page 156, to make 2 mittens; do not turn right side out.

15. For each mitten cuff, repeat Step 13.

16. Stuff each mitten lightly with fiberfill.

17. For belt, spray paint front of buckle; allow to dry. Follow manufacturer's instructions to assemble buckle. Thread belting through buckle.

18. For bag, match right sides and fold fabric piece in half. Using a ½" seam allowance, sew along long edge and 1 short edge. Fold remaining raw edge 7" to wrong side; press. Stitch close to raw edge; turn bag right side out. Fill bag ⅔ full with tissue paper.

19. To provide support for head, wire dowel to center support of tree near top.

20. (**Note:** Refer to photo for Steps 20 – 24.) To decorate tree, hang garland from top to lower branches of tree, spacing evenly.

21. Place hat on head and tack in place; wire head to top of tree. Wire bag to 1 side of tree and fill with toys and candy. Wrap rope twice around bag near top; tack ends together in front.

22. Wire 1 mitten around rope; wire remaining mitten at opposite side of tree. With buckle in front, wrap belt around tree; secure with wire at back.

23. For "coat trim," place a thick roll of fiberfill evenly among bottom branches. Cover tree stand with batting. Place boots under tree.

24. Hang glass ball ornaments on tree.

Leave Open

MITTEN

GIANT STUFFED CANDY CANES (Shown on pages 52 and 54)

For each candy cane, you will need two 10" x 17" pieces of white fabric, 1 yd of ⅞"w red grosgrain ribbon, white and red thread, tracing paper, fabric marking pencil, and polyester fiberfill.

1. Matching registration marks (⊕) and overlapping pattern pieces, trace candy cane pattern on this page onto tracing paper and cut out.
2. Leaving openings as shown on pattern, follow **Sewing Shapes**, page 156, to make candy cane from fabric pieces. Do not turn right side out.
3. Referring to **Fig. 1**, tie thread around each end of candy cane 1¾" from raw edge and knot securely. Trim raw edges ½" from thread ties. Turn right side out. Firmly stuff candy cane with fiberfill. Sew final closure by hand.

Fig. 1

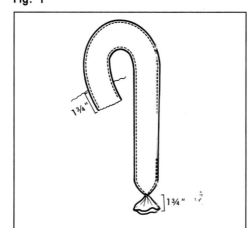

4. Fold 1 end of ribbon ½" to wrong side. Referring to **Fig. 2**, pin folded edge to inside seam of candy cane. Referring to photo, wrap ribbon around candy cane. Fold excess ribbon to wrong side. Trim excess ribbon ½" from fold. Pin folded edge to candy cane. Whipstitch ribbon ends in place.

Fig.2

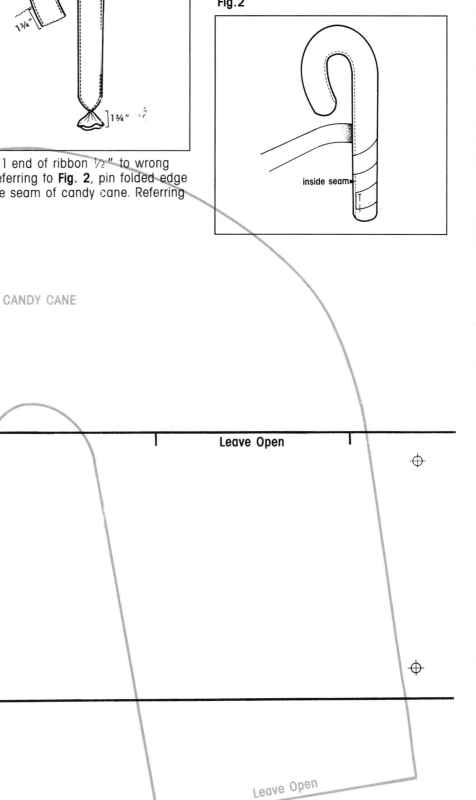

inside seam→

CANDY CANE

Leave Open

Leave Open

Leave Open

FRUITS OF THE SEASON

The beauty of nature is apparent throughout the year, and we delight in finding ways to bring its quiet splendor into our homes for the holidays.

We had only to look around us at nature's magnificent bounty to find the inspiration for this elegant collection. A striking array of natural elements blends together in harmony, creating a majestic mood. A garland of Spanish moss, dressed up with apples, lemons, pinecones, and a variety of dried items, provides a rustic wrap for the tree. Gilded nuts and leaves lend a luxurious dimension, while a rich ruby garland and tree skirt complete the tree's graceful look. The lovely arrangement on the mantel echoes the stately grandeur of the tree, and a bowl of fruit and pinecone potpourri duplicates the tree's warm red and gold tones.

Instructions for the projects shown here and on the next two pages begin on page 68. Take advantage of all that nature has to offer and enjoy the fruits of the season!

Fresh fruit and lush greenery make this beautiful **Buffet Tree** *(page 69)* a special focal point for any room. Placed in a handsome bowl, **Pinecone Potpourri** *(page 68)* is an attractive accent for a table or shelf. Spicy fragrance is added to the pinecones with a dusting of ginger, cinnamon, and dried orange peel.

Our **Fruitful Holiday Wreath** *(page 69)* will add a classic touch to your home's Yuletide finery. Decorated with fruits, dried flowers, nuts, and other natural treasures, the wreath coordinates with the **Fruits of the Season Tree** *(page 68)* and **Mantel Arrangement** *(page 69)* shown on pages 64 and 65.

With an armful of branches and his basket at hand, our **Elegant Santa** *(page 70)* is busy gathering nature's bounty. Dressed for the cold Christmas weather in his fur-trimmed cape and hat, he's sure to stay warm and cozy.

FRUITS OF THE SEASON TREE (Shown on page 65)

A beautiful cornucopia of the finest that nature has to offer is swirled among the branches of this Fruits of the Season Tree. Used as ornaments, fresh fruit, nuts, and dried materials in lovely shades of red, yellow, green, and gold make a striking visual impact.

Working with Natural Materials (on this page) provides instructions on how to prepare and attach these natural ornaments to the tree.

To decorate the tree, wind Spanish Moss Garland (on this page) around the tree. To provide anchors for heavy items such as fruit, create "nests" of floral foam. Cover 6" x 3" x 1" blocks of floral foam with Spanish moss and secure with floral pins or U-shaped pieces of wire. The blocks can then be wired to the branches of the tree behind the moss garland. Apples and lemons are the first to be attached to the foam blocks; nuts and sponge mushrooms can then be secured.

Using your own creative flair, arrange items such as dried teasel and yarrow, cedar roses, pinecones, and dried pods by inserting stems or wire picks into the foam around the fruit. Birch twigs, dried chenopodium, gilded leaves, and feathers can be inserted in the branches to create a lacy effect. A small amount of hot glue can sometimes hold an item right where it's needed.

For the final touch, weave Shirred Garland (page 70) and ⅜" dia. hemp rope among the moss garland and arrangements.

To complete this luxurious still life, drape several yards of red fabric around the base of the tree. The result is a combination of nature's best that will bring you and yours a truly fruitful Christmas.

WORKING WITH NATURAL MATERIALS

PREPARING MATERIALS

Use the following steps to prepare the natural materials for use in the projects.

1. Keep fruit refrigerated until ready for use.
2. Condition greenery by recutting stems 1" above the original cut. For woody stems, split stems 1" or 2" from ends. Place greenery ends in warm water for 8 to 24 hours.
3. Spray walnuts and dried leaves with metallic gold paint; allow to dry.

ATTACHING MATERIALS

For arrangement of natural materials, refer to photos for placement suggestions and then use your own creative instincts to design arrangements that are uniquely your own. Items can be secured in arrangements by following the instructions below.

1. To attach fruit to a floral foam block, insert a 4" long wooden floral pick 1½" into the fruit; insert the pick into the foam.
2. To attach fruit to a wire base, insert an 18" length of 22-gauge florist wire through the fruit; bend ends of wire down (**Fig. 1**) and attach to form.

Fig. 1

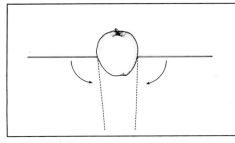

3. To attach nuts or pinecones, form a small loop in 1 end of an 8" length of florist wire. Hot glue wire loop to nut or pinecone. Insert wire into foam or wrap wire around a branch or wire base to secure.
4. Insert items such as twigs, dried flowers, feathers, leaves, sponge mushrooms, and cedar roses securely into arrangement or branches; hot glue items in place if necessary.
5. Use wire cutters to trim excess wire.

PRESERVING MATERIALS

Arrangements using fresh fruit and greenery have a limited life span and are best saved for special occasions. The life of fresh arrangements may be extended by following a few simple steps below.

1. Prepare the project as close as possible to the day of display.
2. After completing the project, spray leaves of greenery with an antidesiccant (available at floral shops or garden centers). A spray bottle filled with acrylic floor wax may be substituted for antidesiccant.
3. To store a small arrangement, place arrangement on layers of wet newspapers in a plastic bag. Seal bag and refrigerate. Remove from bag when ready to display.
4. To store a large arrangement, place arrangement in a cool location such as an unheated garage until ready to display.
5. When displaying an arrangement, keep the arrangement away from dry heat as much as possible; turn the heat down in the room where the arrangement is displayed.
6. If fruit begins to spoil, immediately remove fruit from arrangement and replace with fresh fruit.

PINECONE POTPOURRI
(Shown on page 66)

You will need pinecones, craft glue, foam brush, ground ginger, ground cinnamon, dried orange peel, apples, lemons, fresh greenery (we used fresh huckleberry from a local florist), Spanish moss, dried yarrow, walnuts painted gold, assorted nuts, cedar roses (available at floral or craft shops), and desired container.

1. Mix 1 part glue to 1 part water.
2. Use foam brush to coat pinecones with glue mixture.
3. Mix equal parts of each spice in a small bowl. Sprinkle spice mixture over pinecones, coating well; allow to dry.
4. Fill container with Spanish moss. Referring to photo, arrange pinecones, apples, lemons, greenery, yarrow, cedar roses, and nuts in container.

SPANISH MOSS GARLAND
(Shown on page 65)

You will need Spanish moss, 18-gauge spool wire, hot glue gun, and glue sticks.

1. (**Note:** Repeat Steps 1 – 3 to make desired number of garland lengths.) Cut a 3 yd length of wire.
2. Pull small pieces of moss from larger moss piece.
3. Apply glue to approximately 5" of wire; being careful to avoid contact with hot glue, quickly wrap small moss pieces around glued portion of wire. Repeat to cover wire completely.

BUFFET TREE (Shown on page 66)

You will need one 42"h wire tomato stand, Spanish moss, 10 yds of ⅜" dia. hemp rope, fresh greenery (we used huckleberry from a local florist), fresh fruit (we used plums, strawberries, and Bosc pears), nuts (we used walnuts, hazelnuts, and buckeyes), dried leaves, pinecones, 22-gauge florist wire, wire cutters, one 36" x 42" piece of chicken wire, metallic gold spray paint, hot glue gun, glue sticks, and antidesiccant or a spray bottle filled with acrylic floor wax.

1. Before beginning tree, follow Preparing Materials instructions (Working with Natural Materials), page 68.
2. For tree form, refer to **Fig. 1** and bend each prong of tomato stand 6" to inside of stand; wire prongs together to form a point.

Fig. 1

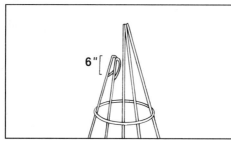

3. (**Note:** Wear gloves to protect hands when working with chicken wire.) Wrap form with chicken wire. Use small pieces of florist wire to secure chicken wire to form (**Fig. 2**). Use wire cutters to trim chicken wire as necessary.

Fig. 2

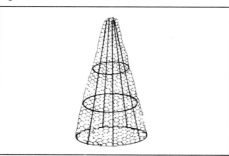

4. (**Note:** Refer to photo for Steps 4 – 7.) Beginning at bottom of tree form and working toward the top, use wire to attach stems of greenery to tree form.
5. For rope garland, paint rope; allow to dry. Cut two 4 yd lengths from rope. Wrap pieces of moss around 1 length. Twist moss-covered length with remaining 4 yd length; glue ends to secure. Arrange rope garland around tree; wire to secure.
6. Cut remaining rope in half. Tie pieces together into a bow. Wire bow to top of tree.
7. Follow Attaching Materials and Preserving Materials instructions (Working with Natural Materials), page 68, to complete and preserve tree.

MANTEL ARRANGEMENT (Shown on pages 64 and 65)

You will need Spanish moss, fresh greenery (we used fresh huckleberry from a local florist), apples, lemons, nuts (we used walnuts, hazelnuts, and buckeyes), dried leaves, birch twigs, pinecones, dried floral items (we used sponge mushrooms, dried chenopodium, and dried yarrow from a local florist), one 2" x 4" x 8" block of floral foam for base, 22-gauge florist wire, green crepe florist tape, wire cutters, 4" floral picks, floral pins (U-shaped pins), metallic gold spray paint, hot glue gun, glue sticks, antidesiccant or a spray bottle filled with acrylic floor wax, and newspapers and a large plastic bag (optional).

1. Before beginning arrangement, follow Preparing Materials instructions (Working with Natural Materials), page 68.
2. For base, pin Spanish moss to top, front, and sides of foam block using floral pins or small pieces of wire bent into U-shapes.
3. Refer to photo and insert greenery stems into foam base, covering top, front, and sides.
4. For branches extending from sides of arrangement, twist several pieces of florist wire together to form a thicker wire. Tape a branch of greenery to 1 end of twisted wire (**Fig. 1**). Insert remaining end of wire securely into foam base. Repeat as necessary to create desired shape.

Fig. 1

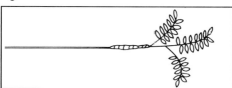

5. Follow Attaching Materials and Preserving Materials instructions (Working with Natural Materials), page 68, to complete and preserve arrangement.

FRUITFUL HOLIDAY WREATH
(Shown on page 67)

You will need desired greenery (we used fresh huckleberry from a local florist), apples, lemons, walnuts, dried leaves, birch twigs, pinecones, dried floral items (we used sponge mushrooms, dried teasel, dried chenopodium, and dried yarrow from a local florist), one 17" dia. wire wreath form, wire cutters, 22-gauge florist wire, metallic gold spray paint, hot glue gun, glue sticks, antidesiccant or a spray bottle filled with acrylic floor wax, and newspapers and a large plastic bag (optional).

1. Before beginning wreath, follow Preparing Materials instructions (Working with Natural Materials), page 68.
2. To make horseshoe-shaped wreath form, refer to **Fig. 1** and use wire cutters to cut a section from top of wreath form.

Fig. 1

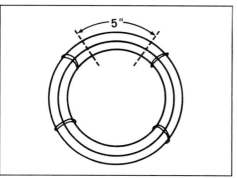

3. To attach greenery, refer to **Fig. 2** and use florist wire to secure pieces of greenery to wreath form, beginning at ends and working toward the bottom. Trim excess wire.

Fig. 2

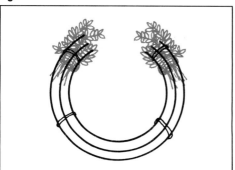

4. Follow Attaching Materials and Preserving Materials instructions (Working with Natural Materials), page 68, to complete and preserve wreath.

SHIRRED GARLAND

(Shown on page 65)

You will need ¾" dia. cotton cord 18" longer than desired length of finished garland, one 4"w strip of fabric twice as long as desired length of finished garland (pieced as necessary), and thread to match fabric.

1. Measure 18" from 1 end of cord and mark with a pin. Place 1 end of fabric strip right side up on a flat surface. Refer to **Fig. 1** to place marked end of cord on fabric strip. With cord centered, fold long edges of strip over cord and securely tack end of fabric strip to cord.

Fig. 1

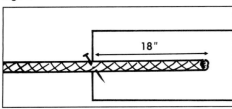

2. Using a ¼" seam allowance and beginning at tacked end of fabric strip, sew long edges of fabric strip together over cord for approximately 15". Leaving needle in fabric and raising presser foot, gently pull cord toward you (**Fig. 2**) and slide fabric back over itself until approximately 12" of fabric strip is pushed over tacked end of fabric and turned right side out. Being careful not to push fabric beyond opposite end of cord, lower presser foot and continue to sew and turn fabric strip at 15" intervals to end of fabric strip. At end of fabric strip, securely tack fabric to cord.

Fig. 2

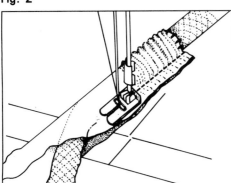

3. Cut off excess 18" of cord. Whipstitch each end of fabric closed over end of cord. Adjust fabric gathers evenly along cord.

ELEGANT SANTA (Shown on page 67)

You will need ⅞ yd of 44"w fabric for coat and hat; one 4" square of beige polyester suede for beard; one 4½" x 7½" piece of beige polyester suede for face; four 3" squares of fabric for mittens; string; removable fabric marking pen; thumbtack or pin; liquid fray preventative (optional); one approx. 8" x 15" piece of rabbit fur for coat and hat trim; white raw wool for beard (available at craft stores); fabric glue; craft knife; paring knife; 17" of 18-gauge wire; masking tape; two 5" squares of craft batting; polyester fiberfill; small crochet hook (optional); tracing paper; 3" long plastic foam egg; empty 2-liter plastic soft drink bottle with cap; hot glue gun; glue sticks; small rubber band; thread to match fabrics and raw wool; approx. 2 cups of bird gravel; 1 skein each of red, green, and gold embroidery floss; and desired items to decorate Santa (we used fresh greenery, twigs, dried chenopodium, and a small basket filled with greenery, dried flowers and berries, feathers, and pinecones).

1. For coat, cut a 27" square from fabric. Fold fabric in half from top to bottom and again from left to right.
2. To mark outer cutting line, tie 1 end of string to fabric marking pen. Insert thumbtack through string 11¾" from pen. Insert thumbtack in fabric as shown in **Fig. 1** and mark ¼ of a circle.

Fig. 1

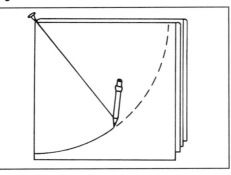

3. To mark inner cutting line, repeat Step 2, inserting thumbtack through string ½" from fabric marking pen.
4. (**Note:** To prevent fraying of raw edges when working with coat and hat fabric, zigzag stitch close to all cut edges of fabric or follow manufacturer's instructions to apply liquid fray preventative to edges.) Following cutting lines and cutting through all thicknesses of fabric, cut out coat.

5. For coat sleeves, cut a 5½" x 19" piece from fabric. Matching right sides and raw edges, fold piece in half lengthwise. Use a ¼" seam allowance and sew long edges together to form a tube. Turn right side out.

6. Referring to **Fig. 2**, place tube on a flat surface and use fabric marking pen to mark cutting line at each end of tube. Cutting through all thicknesses of fabric, cut along marked lines.

Fig. 2

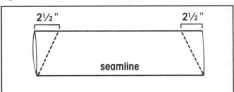

2½"   2½"

seamline

7. Referring to **Fig. 3**, wrap each batting piece securely around wire, leaving 3" of wire at center uncovered; securely tape in place.

Fig. 3

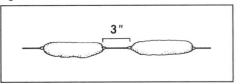

3"

8. Insert padded wire into sleeve. (If batting pieces slip, use crochet hook to position them back in place.)
9. Trace mitten pattern, page 71, onto tracing paper and cut out. Follow **Sewing Shapes**, page 156, to make 2 mittens from fabric squares. Stuff mittens lightly with fiberfill. Place 1 mitten over each end of wire; securely tape raw edges to wire.
10. For head, refer to **Fig. 4** and use paring knife to cut 1" from plastic foam egg.

Fig. 4

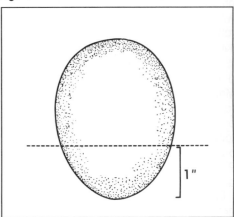

1"

11. Center bottle cap on cut end of egg; press lightly to make an indentation in egg. Remove cap and use paring knife to carve out indentation to fit over cap. Hot glue top of cap to inside of egg.

12. (**Note:** Use fabric glue to assemble Santa in Steps 12 – 22.) Apply glue to 1 long edge on wrong side of face fabric. Referring to **Fig. 5a**, place glued edge of face fabric along cut edge of egg. Leaving excess fabric extending above top of egg, wrap fabric around egg, overlapping short edges. Allow to dry. Gather excess fabric close to top of egg; secure with rubber band (**Fig. 5b**).

Fig. 5a

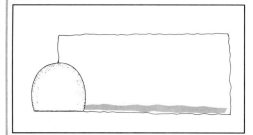

Fig. 5b

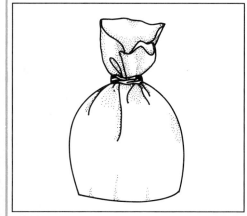

13. For beard, use beard pattern and follow **Transferring Patterns**, page 156. Cut 1 beard piece from fabric. Refer to photo and tack small pieces of raw wool to 1 side of beard piece, covering fabric completely.

14. For hat, use hat pattern and follow **Transferring Patterns**, page 156. Use pattern and cut 1 hat piece from fabric. Matching right sides and straight edges, fold hat in half. Use a ¼ " seam allowance and sew straight edges together. Clip corner and turn right side out. Baste ½ " from raw edge of hat. Pull basting thread, gathering hat to fit around head. Place approximately 1 tablespoon of bird gravel into tip of hat. Refer to photo and glue edge of hat

to head approximately 1¼ " from bottom edge of head; allow to dry.

15. (**Note:** When cutting fur strips, use a **very** sharp craft knife. Do not use scissors. Cut carefully through back of fur piece only.) For trim at bottom of coat, cut ½ " wide strips of fur to form a strip approximately 74" long. With nap of fur strips facing the same direction, refer to photo and glue fur strips along bottom edge of coat; allow to dry.

16. For trim at front of coat, cut a ½ " x 10½ " strip of fur. Glue trim along 1 fold line of coat; allow to dry.

17. Cut two ½ " x 7" strips of fur. Glue strips along edges of sleeve openings; allow to dry. Referring to photo, glue bottom edges of each sleeve opening together; allow to dry.

18. Cut a ½ " x 9" strip of fur. Glue strip along bottom edge of hat; allow to dry.

19. Cut a small scrap of fur and form into a small ball. Glue to tip of hat; allow to dry.

20. Fill bottle with remaining gravel. Place coat over bottle. Twist head onto bottle. Turn coat so that front fur trim is at center front.

21. Position arms across the back of coat close to neck of bottle (**Fig. 6**). Whipstitch arms in place. Refer to photo to position arms.

Fig. 6

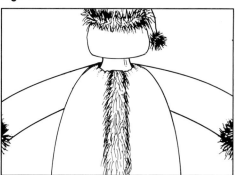

22. For hair, wrap a piece of raw wool around base of head; glue to secure. Glue beard to front of head; allow to dry.

23. For cape, cut a 3" x 15" piece of fur. Refer to photo to position fur piece around shoulders; tack in place.

24. For belt, cut four 2 yd lengths of floss from each color. Matching ends, place lengths together. Knot lengths together 2" from 1 end; repeat for remaining end. Fasten 1 end to a stationary object. Pull floss taut and twist tightly. Matching knotted ends, fold floss in half and allow to twist together; knot ends together to secure. Pull cord through fingers to evenly distribute twists. Knot cord 2½ " from each end. Trim each end 2" from knot; fringe ends. Refer to photo to tie belt around Santa.

25. Refer to photo to decorate Santa.

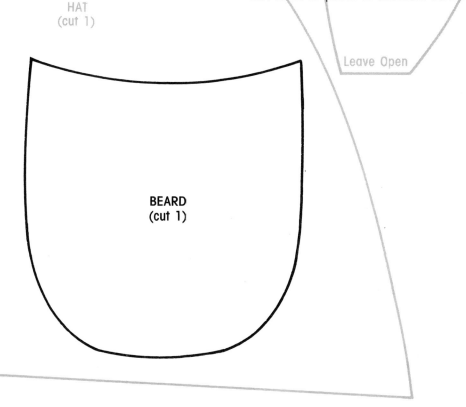

HAT
(cut 1)

Leave Open

BEARD
(cut 1)

JOURNEY TO BETHLEHEM

As we celebrate the joyous Christmas season, the beloved events of the first Noel are retold with reverence and grace. From simple Nativities to elaborate works of art, we find new ways to share this special story. Cross stitched with tender care, each of the sampler-style ornaments in this impressive collection bears glad tidings of the birth of Christ. Their quiet simplicity reminds us of His humble beginnings. The miracle that awaited Mary and Joseph at the end of their long journey to Bethlehem is truly reason to rejoice this Christmas — and every Christmas!

The delicate **Nativity Scherenschnitte** *(page 74)*, with its message of peace and love, leads us to reflect on the significance of the Christmas celebration. Heralded by angels, the tiny Baby's birth brought great joy to the world.

Beautiful **Sampler Ornaments** *(page 74)* edged with elegant twisted cord are the focal point of the lovely **Journey to Bethlehem Tree** *(page 74)*. The linen ornaments are cross stitched with eight different messages, each telling a small portion of the Christmas story. Clustered throughout the tree, richly colored berries, ivy, and other natural elements make an attractive backdrop for the samplers.

JOURNEY TO BETHLEHEM TREE

(Shown on page 73)

Elegant in its simplicity and reverent in its message, this Journey to Bethlehem Tree illustrates the true meaning of Christmas.

Exquisite cross-stitched Sampler Ornaments (on this page) are rich in beauty and color. Crafted from classic linen and encircled with graceful twisted cording fashioned from embroidery floss, these ornaments are sure to become treasured heirlooms.

Completing the tree are simple elements of nature that echo and enhance the warm hues of the ornaments. Sprigs of dried pepper grass and statice create golden nests of color among the boughs. A variety of artificial berries add a crimson glow. Weaving around the tree, vines of artificial ivy provide a striking and unusual finish for this lovely tree.

NATIVITY SCHERENSCHNITTE (Shown on page 72)

You will need one 11" x 14" piece of parchment scherenschnitte paper; craft knife; cutting mat or a thick layer of newspapers; desired color mat board; spray adhesive; desired frame (we used a custom frame); and matte clear acrylic spray or tracing paper, graphite transfer paper, and removable tape.

1. (**Note:** Follow Step 1 to transfer pattern to scherenschnitte paper **or** photocopy design directly onto scherenschnitte paper and spray lightly with acrylic spray to prevent photocopy ink from smearing.) Trace pattern onto tracing paper. Center pattern on 1 side (wrong side) of scherenschnitte paper and tape 1 edge in place. Place transfer paper, coated side down, under tracing paper. Holding papers in place, draw over lines of pattern to transfer pattern onto scherenschnitte paper. Remove pattern and transfer paper.

2. Place scherenschnitte paper on cutting mat. Beginning at center of design and working to outer edges, use craft knife to cut out design. Cut small areas first, larger areas next, and outer edges last.

3. Cut mat board 1" larger on all sides than scherenschnitte. Apply spray adhesive to wrong side of scherenschnitte. Carefully position scherenschnitte on mat board, guiding loose areas of scherenschnitte into place. Press firmly to secure.

4. Trim matted scherenschnitte to desired size and insert in frame.

SAMPLER ORNAMENTS   (Shown on page 73)

For each ornament, you will need two 8" squares of Raw Belfast Linen (32 ct), embroidery floss (see color key, page 76), embroidery hoop (optional), 2 skeins of embroidery floss for twisted cord (we used DMC 815 for red cord, DMC 680 for gold cord, and DMC 924 for blue cord), craft glue, fabric marking pencil, thread to match fabric and floss for twisted cord, and polyester fiberfill.

1. Follow **Working On Linen**, page 156, to work desired design, page 76 or 77, over 2 fabric threads on 1 fabric square. Use 2 strands of floss for Cross Stitch.
2. Place stitched piece and remaining fabric square right sides together. Referring to photo for shape, use fabric marking pencil to draw stitching line approximately ½" from stitched design. Leaving an opening for turning, sew fabric squares together directly on pencil line. Trim seam allowance to ⅜"

and clip curves and corners. Turn right side out and press. Stuff ornament with fiberfill; sew final closure by hand.
3. For twisted cord, cut five 2 yd lengths from floss. Matching ends, place lengths together. Knot lengths together 2" from 1 end; repeat for remaining end. Fasten 1 end to a stationary object. Pull floss taut and twist tightly. Matching knotted ends, fold floss in half and allow to twist together; knot ends together to secure. Pull cord through fingers to evenly distribute twists.
4. (**Note:** To prevent cord from untwisting when cut, apply glue to area to be cut. Allow to dry before cutting cord.) Referring to **Fig. 1** and beginning at bottom center of ornament, start ½" from 1 end of twisted cord and tack cord over seam to top center of ornament. For hanger, form a 1" loop of cord at top center of ornament; tack base of loop to seam to secure. Tack

cord over remainder of seam to bottom center of ornament. Trim excess cord to ½". Fold 1 end of twisted cord over the other end and tack ends to back of ornament (**Fig. 1**).

Fig. 1

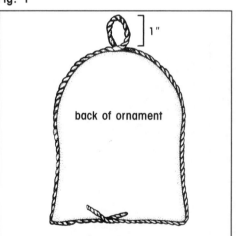

back of ornament

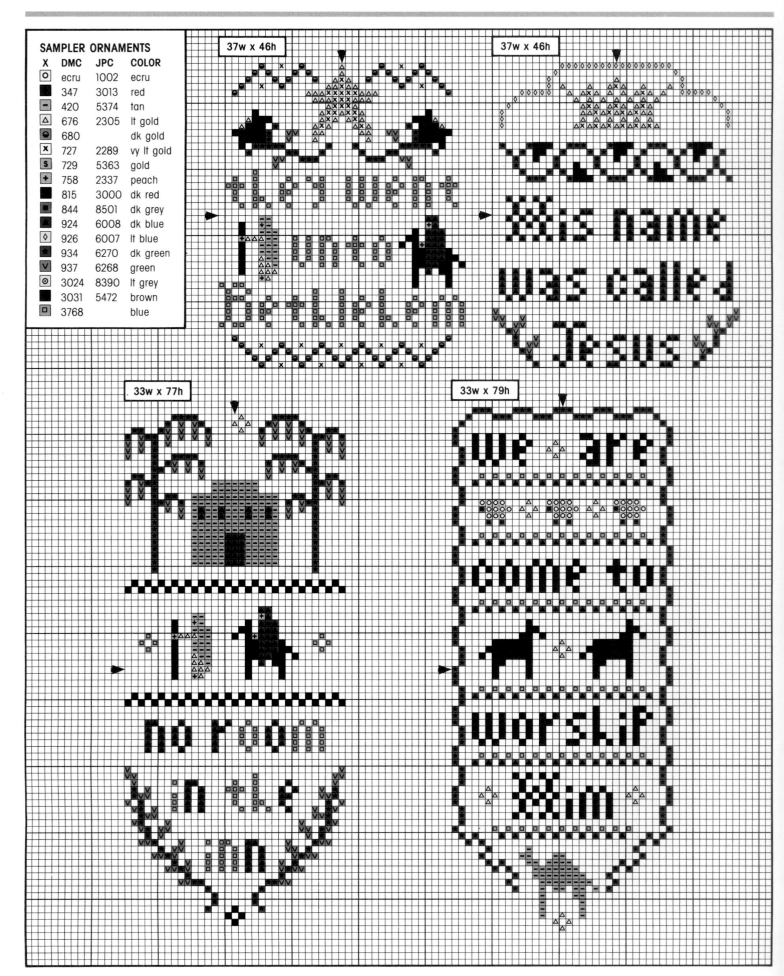

A COZY COUNTRY CHRISTMAS

In Colonial times, the keeping room was the heart and soul of the country home — a cozy gathering place for family, friends, and neighbors. The comforting heat of the fire, the delicious smells drifting from the hearth kettle, and the pleasant sounds of lively conversation created an inviting atmosphere. Warm and welcoming, this cheerful collection evokes the spirit of comfort and hospitality found in the keeping room of yesteryear. Many of the elements used in the decorations are from the pantry, and antique butter molds inspired us to create the wonderful stenciled ornaments. Our three butter mold motifs were chosen for their symbolism: the cow for richness of life, the flower for happiness, and the wheat for abundance. Instructions for the projects shown here and on the next two pages begin on page 82. Enjoy a cozy country Christmas!

Filled with holiday greenery and other trimmings, this **Homespun Oven Mitt** *(page 84)* makes a merry Christmas door decoration.

78

From the **Cinnamon Treetop Star** *(page 83)* to the quilted **Pinwheel Tree Skirt** *(page 85)*, the **Cozy Country Tree** *(page 82)* has plenty of Early American charm. **Butter Mold Ornaments** *(page 86)* and **Country Copper Star Ornaments** *(page 83)* share the tree branches with **Cinnamon Stick Icicles** *(page 85)*, **Dried Apple and Orange Ornaments** *(page 82)*, a **Pretzel Garland** *(page 85)*, and other homey touches.

(Opposite) Made of fabrics that coordinate with the tree skirt, **Strip-Quilted Place Mats** (page 84) and matching napkins set the table for a cozy holiday meal. The festive **Star Napkin Rings** (page 82) echo the copper and dried fruit ornaments found on the tree. Candles nestled in beds of cinnamon sticks and cloves will add fragrance to the air, and **Cinnamon Stick Candle Holders** (page 86) will kindle warm feelings.

A cheerful addition to door or window, our **Spicy Country Wreath** (page 86) will delight family and friends. It's sprinkled with ornaments from the tree and adorned with a jolly bow.

COZY COUNTRY TREE

(Shown on page 79)

This delightful Cozy Country Tree warms the kitchen with holiday spirit. Simple items from the kitchen and pantry convert easily into attractive ornaments the whole family will enjoy making.

The Pretzel Garland (page 85) is quick to create and makes a great project for children. Red wooden bead and popcorn garlands are wound around the tree along with the pretzel garland. We used artificial garlands, but stringing garlands of freshly popped popcorn and crisp red cranberries is a project the whole family can enjoy on a cold winter's night.

Inspired by designs carved in antique wooden butter molds, our Butter Mold Ornaments (page 86) recreate the same warmth and charm with paint and stencils.

Christmas lights aren't necessary with the reflections from the lustrous copper ornaments hanging on the tree. Shining from the top of the tree is a bright Cinnamon Treetop Star (page 83). Measuring out doses of good cheer, copper measuring spoons make clever ornaments from the kitchen. The purchased spoons are tied to the tree branches with ½" x 7" strips of torn fabric. Spiky Country Copper Star Ornaments (page 83) are a variation of the treetop star.

For a "tasteful" touch, scatter Dried Apple and Orange Ornaments (on this page) among the branches. Cinnamon Stick Icicles (page 85) created from large sticks of cinnamon and spirals of orange peel provide a spicy fragrance. To finish the tree, clusters of golden rye (purchased from a floral shop or craft store) are tied to the branches with torn 1" x 12" strips of fabric.

A quilted Pinwheel Tree Skirt (page 85) swirls under the tree to complete the picture. Usually a quilt would take many hours to make, but our instructions are fast and easy, and the result is fabulous!

DRIED APPLE ORNAMENTS

(Shown on page 79)

You will need apples (we used Granny Smith apples), lemon juice, salt, paring knife, wire cake racks, tracing paper, matte clear acrylic spray, paper towels, and nylon line (for hangers).

1. (**Note:** We only used slices that contained a part of the core; each apple will yield only 3 or 4 of these slices.) For each apple, cut ¼" thick slices from apple as shown in **Fig. 1**.

Fig. 1

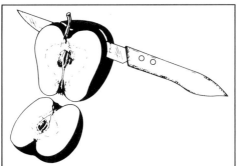

2. Making sure apples are completely covered, soak slices for 20 minutes in a mixture of 2 cups of lemon juice and 3 tablespoons of salt. Remove slices from mixture and blot with paper towels to remove excess moisture. Place slices on wire cake racks in a 150 degree oven. Dry for approximately 6 hours; turn slices over if edges begin to curl. When dried, slices should be pliable and have a leathery feel.
3. For star cutouts, trace apple star pattern onto tracing paper and cut out. Center pattern on dried apple slice; use paring knife to cut around pattern. Remove star-shaped center.
4. Spray each side of apple slices and star cutouts with 2 coats of acrylic spray, allowing to dry between coats.
5. For hangers on apple slices, thread 6" of nylon line through top of each slice and knot ends of line together.

DRIED ORANGE ORNAMENTS

(Shown on page 79)

You will need oranges, wire cake racks, paring knife, matte clear acrylic spray, and nylon line (for hangers).

1. Cut each orange crosswise into ¼" thick slices; discard end pieces.
2. Place slices on wire cake racks in a 150 degree oven. Dry for approximately 6 hours; turn slices over if edges begin to curl. When dried, slices should be pliable.
3. Cut each slice in half. Spray each side of orange slices with 2 coats of acrylic spray, allowing to dry between coats.
4. For hangers, refer to photo and thread 6" of nylon line through top of each slice; knot ends of line together.

STAR NAPKIN RINGS

(Shown on page 81)

For each napkin ring, you will need copper sheeting (available at craft stores), dried apple star cutout (Dried Apple Ornaments, on this page), liquid solder (available at hardware stores), tracing paper, utility scissors, spring-type clothespin, hot glue gun, and glue sticks.

1. (**Note:** Cut edges of copper may be sharp.) For napkin ring, cut one 1½" x 7" piece of copper. Form strip into a ring, overlapping ends 1". Following manufacturer's instructions, solder ends of strip together; use clothespin to secure. Allow solder to dry; remove clothespin.
2. For star, trace copper star pattern, page 83, onto tracing paper and cut out. Use pattern and cut 1 star from copper.
3. Referring to photo, follow manufacturer's instructions to solder star to ring; use clothespin to secure. Allow solder to dry; remove clothespin.
4. Refer to photo and glue apple cutout to center of star.

APPLE STAR

COUNTRY COPPER STAR ORNAMENTS

(Shown on page 79)

For each ornament, you will need one 5" square of copper sheeting (available at craft stores), five 2¼" long cinnamon sticks, one ½" dia. artificial berry, tracing paper, utility scissors, hot glue gun, glue sticks, and 6" of nylon line (for hanger).

1. Trace copper star pattern onto tracing paper and cut out.
2. (**Note:** Cut edges of copper may be sharp.) Use pattern and cut 1 star from copper.
3. Referring to photo, glue berry to center of star; glue cinnamon sticks to star.
4. For hanger, match ends of nylon line and fold in half to form a loop; knot ends together. Glue knot to back of ornament at top of 1 cinnamon stick.

CINNAMON TREETOP STAR

(Shown on page 79)

You will need one 8½" square of copper sheeting (available at craft stores), utility scissors, dried apple star cutout (Dried Apple Ornaments, page 82), ten 2" long cinnamon sticks, five 1¾" long cinnamon sticks, tracing paper, hot glue gun, and glue sticks.

1. Use treetop star pattern and follow

Transferring Patterns, page 156.
2. (**Note:** Cut edges of copper may be sharp.) Use pattern and cut 1 star from copper.
3. Referring to photo, glue 2" long cinnamon sticks to star along outside edges; glue remaining cinnamon sticks to star. Glue apple cutout to star.

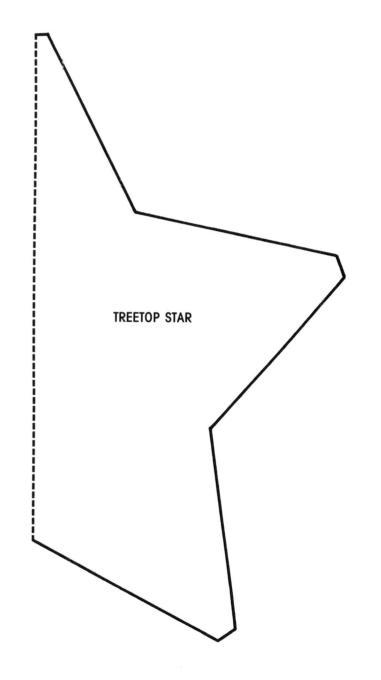

COPPER STAR

TREETOP STAR

STRIP-QUILTED PLACE MATS (Shown on page 81)

For each place mat, you will need nine 2½" x 20" strips of fabric in coordinating colors, one 16" x 20" piece of fabric for backing, one 2" x 70" bias strip of fabric to match backing (pieced as necessary), one 16" x 20" piece of polyester bonded batting, removable fabric marking pen, and thread to match fabrics.

1. Place backing fabric wrong side up on a flat surface. Matching edges, place batting on backing fabric.

2. (Note: Use a ½" seam allowance for Steps 2 and 3.) Matching long edges, place one 20" long strip right side up on batting. Referring to **Fig. 1**, sew all layers together along top edge of strip.

Fig. 1

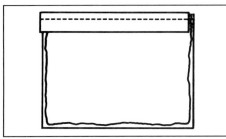

3. Referring to **Fig. 2**, match right sides and raw edges and place top edge of second strip along bottom edge of first strip. Stitch through all layers of place mat **(Fig. 2)**. Fold second strip down over batting and press. Repeat for remaining strips.

Fig. 2

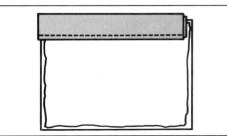

4. Use fabric marking pen to mark a 14" x 19" rectangle in center of quilted piece. Machine baste along pen line. Trim fabric ¼" from stitched line.

5. For binding, match wrong sides and raw edges and fold bias strip in half lengthwise; press. Open 1 end of binding; press end ¼" to wrong side. Refold binding strip. Beginning with pressed end and matching right sides and raw edges, pin binding to place mat. Using a ¼" seam allowance, sew binding to place mat.

6. Cut corners diagonally and press binding to back of place mat; whipstitch in place.

HOMESPUN OVEN MITT (Shown on page 78)

You will need an ecru cotton oven mitt, one 5" x 30" strip of torn fabric for cuff, thread to match cuff fabric, fabric marking pencil, one 2" x 3" x 6" block of floral foam, fresh or artificial greenery, sprays of artificial berries, stalks of dried rye (available at craft stores or floral shops), Cinnamon Stick Icicles (page 85), and 8" of florist wire (for hanger).

1. Referring to **Fig. 1**, use fabric marking pencil to draw a straight line across mitt. Cutting through all layers, cut along pencil line.

Fig. 1

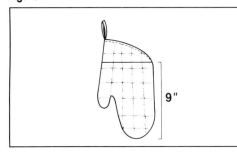

2. Turn oven mitt wrong side out. Mark center of 1 long edge of fabric strip with a pin. Matching right side of fabric strip to wrong side of mitt, place marked center of strip at top edge of mitt at thumb seamline. Referring to **Fig. 2**, pin strip to raw edge of mitt.

Fig. 2

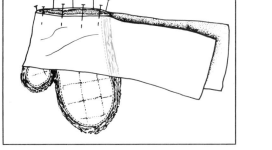

3. Use a ½" seam allowance and sew strip to mitt. Turn mitt right side out and fold cuff down over mitt. Knot ends of cuff close to mitt and tack knot to mitt below cuff seam.

4. Insert floral foam into mitt. Referring to photo, insert greenery, berries, rye, and icicles into mitt.

5. For hanger, thread wire through top center on back of mitt.

PINWHEEL TREE SKIRT (Shown on page 79)

You will need fifty-six 2½" x 22" strips of fabric in coordinating colors (we used 11 different fabrics), four 22" squares of fabric for backing, one 2"w bias strip of fabric 6¼ yds long to match backing (pieced as necessary), four 22" squares of polyester bonded batting, compass, and thread to match fabrics.

1. Follow Steps 1 — 3 of Strip-Quilted Place Mats instructions, page 84, to sew fourteen 22" long strips to each of the backing fabric squares.
2. Referring to **Fig. 1**, cut each quilted square in half diagonally.

Fig. 1

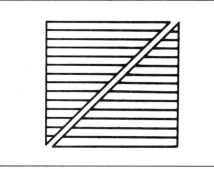

3. Referring to **Fig. 2**, match right sides and raw edges and use a ½" seam allowance to sew 1 short edge of 1 triangle piece to long edge of another triangle piece. Press seam open.

Fig. 2

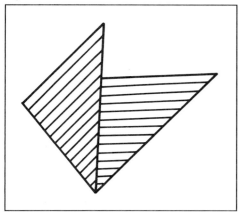

4. Referring to **Fig. 3** and leaving opening as shown, repeat Step 3 to sew remaining triangle pieces together.

Fig. 3

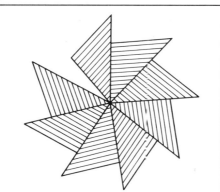

5. For center opening in tree skirt, use compass to draw a 4" dia circle in center of tree skirt; cut along drawn line (**Fig. 4**).

Fig. 4

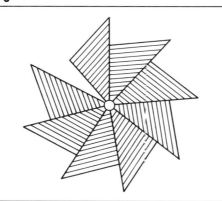

6. For edge of tree skirt, refer to **Fig. 5** and match outer edges and fold point of each triangle piece to 1 side; cut along fold line.

Fig. 5

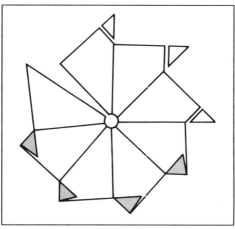

7. For binding, follow Steps 5 and 6 of Strip-Quilted Place Mats instructions, page 84, to bind all raw edges of tree skirt.

PRETZEL GARLAND
(Shown on page 79)

You will need desired fabric, a bag of large Bavarian pretzels, and thread to match fabric.

1. Tear ¾" wide strips from fabric.
2. Matching right sides and short edges, use a ¼" seam allowance and sew 2 strips together; press seam open. Repeat to join fabric strips to make 1 long strip 16" longer than desired length of garland.
3. Refer to **Fig. 1** to weave 1 end of fabric strip through pretzel, tie end of strip to pretzel. Spacing pretzels approximately 3" apart, weave fabric strip through pretzels to within 8" of remaining end of fabric strip. Tie remaining end around last pretzel.

Fig. 1

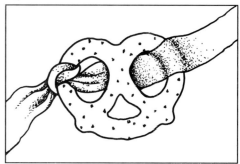

CINNAMON STICK ICICLES
(Shown on page 79)

For each icicle, you will need 1 approx. ⅛" x 8" strip cut from fresh orange peel, 1 approx. 6" long cinnamon stick, 2 spring-type clothespins, hot glue gun, glue sticks, and 6" of nylon line (for hanger).

1. Match 1 end of orange peel strip to 1 end of cinnamon stick. Referring to photo, wrap peel strip around cinnamon stick. Secure each end of peel strip to cinnamon stick with a clothespin; allow peel to dry.
2. Remove clothespins and trim ends of peel even with ends of cinnamon stick if necessary. Glue ends of peel to cinnamon stick.
3. For hanger, match ends of nylon line and fold in half to form a loop; knot ends together. Glue knot to 1 end of cinnamon stick.

CINNAMON STICK CANDLE HOLDER

(Shown on page 81)

You will need 1 clear glass votive candle holder with straight sides, 1 votive candle, approx. 20 cinnamon sticks, transparent tape, utility scissors, hot glue gun, and glue sticks.

1. Measure height of candle holder and add ½"; cut cinnamon sticks the determined measurement.
2. (**Note:** Hot glue will not make a permanent bond on glass.) To provide a surface glue will adhere to, cover outside of candle holder with transparent tape (**Fig. 1**).

Fig. 1

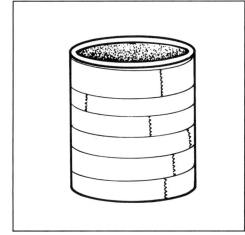

3. Referring to photo, glue cinnamon sticks to candle holder.
4. Insert candle into candle holder.

SPICY COUNTRY WREATH (Shown on page 80)

You will need one 17" dia. artificial evergreen wreath, Country Copper Star Ornaments (page 83; omit hangers), Dried Apple Ornaments (page 82; omit hangers), Dried Orange Ornaments (page 82; omit hangers), Cinnamon Stick Icicles (page 85; omit hangers), one 2" x 39" strip of torn fabric for bow, stalks of dried rye (available at craft stores or floral shops), ½" x 8" strips of torn fabric for dried rye clusters, 22-gauge florist wire, hot glue gun, and glue sticks.

1. (**Note:** Refer to photo for Steps 1 − 3.) Tie 39" fabric strip into a bow. Wire bow to wreath. Trim ends of bow at an angle.
2. Glue star ornaments, icicles, and dried fruit to wreath.
3. Trim rye stalks to 6". For each rye cluster, refer to photo and use an 8" fabric strip to tie 3 stalks together. Insert clusters into wreath; glue to secure. Insert single stalks of rye into wreath; glue to secure.
4. For hanger, cut an 8" length of wire. Fold wire in half and twist ends together. Wire hanger to top back of wreath.

BUTTER MOLD ORNAMENTS (Shown on page 79)

For each ornament, you will need two 6" squares of unbleached canvas fabric; 12" of cotton worsted weight yarn; 15" of ⅜"w picot-edged braid trim; one 4" square of acetate for stencil (available at craft or art supply stores); permanent felt-tip pen with fine point; craft knife; cutting mat or a thick layer of newspapers; craft glue; gesso; foam brushes; the following colors of Folk Art® acrylic paint: Taffy, Molasses, and Coffee Bean; small stencil brush; paper towels; removable tape (optional); thread to match fabric; a soft cloth; polyester fiberfill; and nylon line (for hanger).

1. Use pen to trace desired stencil pattern, page 87, onto acetate. Place acetate on cutting mat and use craft knife to cut out stencil (**Fig. 1**).

Fig. 1

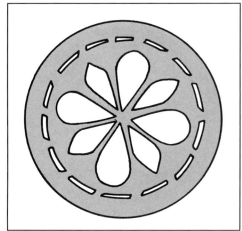

2. Center stencil on 1 canvas square. Using outer edge of stencil as a guideline, use a pencil to draw around stencil; remove stencil. Referring to **Fig. 2**, glue yarn to canvas along pencil line; trim excess yarn. Leaving a ⅛" space between yarn and trim, glue trim to canvas around yarn and trim excess (**Fig. 2**). Allow to dry.

Fig. 2

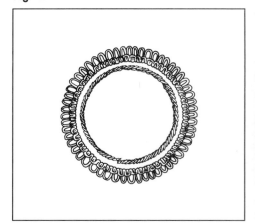

3. Use a pencil to draw a line ⅛" from outside edge of trim. Matching edges, place canvas square trim side up on remaining canvas square. Sew squares together along pencil line. Trim seam allowance to ⅛".
4. Apply 1 coat of gesso to both sides of ornament; allow to dry.
5. Paint both sides of ornament Taffy; allow to dry.
6. Reposition stencil on canvas inside yarn circle. Hold or tape stencil in place while stenciling. Dip dry stencil brush in Coffee Bean and remove excess paint on a paper towel. Brush should be almost dry to produce a good design. Beginning at edge of cutout area, apply paint in a stamping motion. Carefully remove stencil and allow to dry.

7. Mix 1 part Molasses to 1 part water. Use a foam brush to apply diluted paint to ornament. Referring to photo and using a soft cloth, begin at center of ornament and wipe off excess paint, leaving more paint at edges of design. Allow to dry.

8. Repeat Step 7 using Coffee Bean. Allow to dry.

9. Carefully cutting through back of ornament only, cut a 2" long slit in center back of ornament. Stuff ornament lightly with fiberfill; whipstitch opening closed.

10. For hanger, thread 6" of nylon line through top center of ornament and knot ends of line together.

THE SHARING OF CHRISTMAS

The tradition of gift-giving brings great joy to the holiday celebration. Stirred by the spirit of the season, we delight in finding just the right presents for family and friends. Often the gifts we create ourselves are the ones that are most appreciated. Lovingly crafted, they become little reminders of special relationships. Long after the gaily wrapped packages are delivered and opened, our offerings will be treasured for the love they convey.

FESTIVE FLOOR-CLOTH

Painted red and green in celebration of the season, the design on this floorcloth is based on the popular Star of Bethlehem quilt pattern. You'll want to give the decorative mat early so it can be enjoyed all through the holidays.

For a 23" x 38" floorcloth, you will need one 29"x 44" piece of canvas (we used unstretched, unprimed artist's canvas available at craft or art supply stores); tracing paper; red, green, and ivory acrylic paint; foam brushes; small round paintbrush; satin-finish clear polyurethane; tack cloth; gum eraser; graphite transfer paper; craft paper; yardstick; and masking tape.

1. Cover flat work surface with craft paper. Use masking tape to tape edges of canvas to paper.
2. (**Note:** Canvas must be kept flat until it is completely dry. Do not fold floorcloth; paint may crack.) Apply 2 coats of ivory paint to canvas, allowing to dry between coats. Canvas will shrink. Remove paper and tape from dry canvas and press unpainted side of dry canvas with a warm dry iron.
3. Cut a 12" square of tracing paper (pieced as necessary). Fold tracing paper in half from top to bottom and again from left to right. Unfold paper and lay flat. Placing folds of paper along dashed lines of pattern, page 91, trace pattern on ¼ of paper. Repeat for remaining quarters of paper.
4. Referring to grey line on Diagram, use a pencil to mark a line lengthwise along center of floorcloth. Mark center point of line.
5. Referring to Diagram, use transfer paper to transfer pattern twice onto floorcloth.
6. Referring to Diagram, mark borders. Do not cut out.
7. Referring to Diagram, paint red areas of floorcloth; allow to dry. Repeat for green areas.

8. Erase any visible pencil lines on floorcloth. Wipe floorcloth with tack cloth to remove dust. Follow manufacturer's instructions to apply 2 coats of polyurethane to floorcloth, allowing to dry between coats.

9. Trim canvas along outside border. Paint trimmed edges of floorcloth; allow to dry. Apply 1 coat of polyurethane to edges of floorcloth; allow to dry.

10. To clean floorcloth, wipe with a damp cloth. Store floorcloth flat.

DIAGRAM

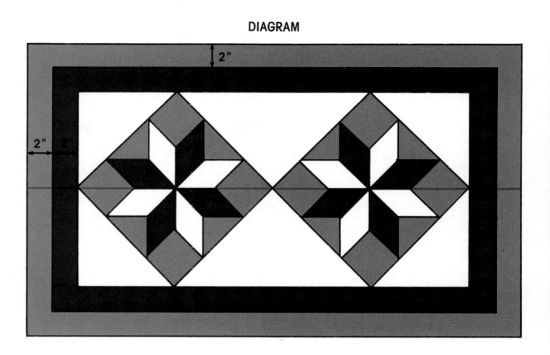

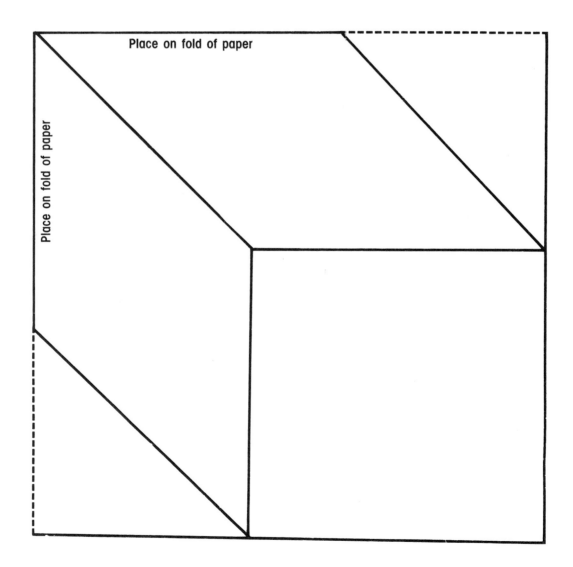

Place on fold of paper

Place on fold of paper

DRESSED-UP GLOVES

Warm, snug gloves are essential winter accessories, and here's a quick and inexpensive way to transform plain ones into festive gifts! Worked in duplicate stitch, our snowflake, horn, and poinsettia designs are easy to add to purchased gloves.

You will need a pair of gloves with a small gauge stockinette stitch (6 — 8 stitches per inch works best), embroidery floss (see color key), #24 tapestry needle, and lightweight cardboard cut to fit snugly inside hand portion of glove.

1. Place cardboard inside 1 glove.
2. Each colored square on the chart indicates 1 Duplicate Stitch (**Figs. 1a** and **1b**). Referring to photo, center and work design on back of glove below ribbed cuff; we used 4 strands of floss. Depending on the gauge of the glove, it may be necessary to increase or decrease the number of strands for adequate coverage.
3. Repeat Steps 1 and 2 for remaining glove.

Duplicate Stitch: To work Duplicate Stitch on gloves, separate strands and thread needle with desired number of strands of floss. With right side facing, bring needle up from wrong side of glove and pull floss through bottom of stitch, leaving a short end on wrong side to weave in later. Needle should always go between strands of yarn. Insert needle from right to left around knit stitch above, keeping floss on top of knit stitch, and pull through (**Fig. 1a**). Insert needle back through bottom of same stitch where Duplicate Stitch began (**Fig. 1b**). Following chart, bring needle up through next stitch and repeat for all charted stitches. Keep tension of stitches even with tension of knitted fabric to avoid puckering. Weave in ends.

Fig. 1a

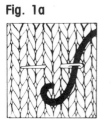

Fig. 1b

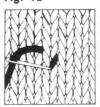

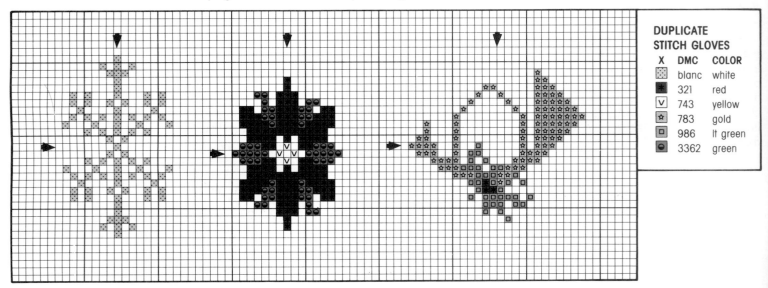

DUPLICATE STITCH GLOVES		
X	**DMC**	**COLOR**
░	blanc	white
✱	321	red
V	743	yellow
☆	783	gold
☐	986	lt green
◉	3362	green

HANDSOME DESK SET

Here's the perfect gift for a man who's going places! Featuring a map motif trimmed with gold braid, this handsome desk set includes a blotter, pencil and paper clip holders, and an address book. For a touch of nostalgia, use a map from a special trip.

For pencil holder, you will need an approx. 4½"h empty can.

For paper clip holder, you will need one 3" x 4" oval Shaker box, foam brush, and glossy Mod Podge® sealer.

For blotter, you will need one 19" x 24" piece of black mat board, two 2½" x 19" pieces of lightweight cardboard, two 2½" x 19" pieces of art foam, and one 18" x 23" piece of desired color charcoal drawing paper (available at art supply stores).

For address book, you will need a purchased address book and spray adhesive.

You will also need road maps, brown Ultra Suede™ fabric (available at specialty fabric stores) and ⅛"w flat gold braid (amounts determined by sizes of projects), Design Master® glossy wood tone spray (available at craft stores), and craft glue.

Note: To prepare maps for projects, press maps with a warm dry iron to remove creases. Spray lightly with wood tone spray. Allow to dry.

PENCIL HOLDER

1. To cover can, measure circumference of can and add 1"; measure height of can. Cut map the determined measurements. Overlapping ends, glue map around can. Allow to dry.

2. For trim, cut one ⅝"w strip and one 1½"w strip from fabric to fit around can.

3. Referring to photo, glue ⅝"w strip along bottom edge of can. With 1 long edge (bottom edge) of 1½"w strip ⅝" from top of can, glue strip around top of can. Glue excess fabric to inside of can. Allow to dry.

4. Cut 2 pieces of braid to fit around can. Refer to photo and center braid on fabric; glue to secure. Allow to dry.

Continued on page 94

PAPER CLIP HOLDER

1. To cover side of box, measure circumference of box and add ½"; measure height of box. Cut map the determined measurements. Overlapping short edges, glue map to box. Allow to dry.
2. To cover box lid, draw around lid on wrong side of map. Cut out map ½" outside pencil line. At ½" intervals, clip edges of map to within ⅛" of pencil line. Center lid on wrong side of map. Glue clipped edges to side of lid. Allow to dry.
3. Apply 2 coats of sealer to box and lid, allowing to dry between coats.
4. For trim, measure width and circumference of side of box lid. Cut a piece of fabric the determined measurements. Cut a piece of braid the same length as fabric. Refer to photo and glue fabric then braid around side of lid. Allow to dry.

BLOTTER

1. For side piece, match edges and glue 1 art foam piece to 1 cardboard piece; allow to dry. Cut a 6½" x 23" piece of map. Place map wrong side up on flat surface. With foam side down, center cardboard on map. Fold 1 long edge of map over cardboard; glue to secure. Allow to dry.
2. Referring to **Fig. 1**, place 1 short edge of mat board along remaining long edge of cardboard piece. Fold edges of map over mat board; glue to secure. Allow to dry.

Fig. 1

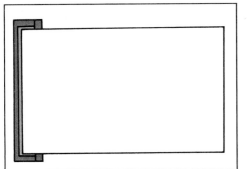

3. Repeat Steps 1 and 2 for remaining side piece.
4. For trim, cut two ⅝" x 23" pieces of fabric and two 23" lengths of gold braid. Beginning 2" from 1 end of fabric, refer to photo and glue fabric strips to side pieces ½" from inner edge; glue ends to back of blotter. Beginning 2" from 1 end, refer to photo and glue braid along center of fabric; glue ends of braid to back of blotter. Allow to dry.
5. Insert charcoal paper into blotter.

ADDRESS BOOK

1. To cover front of book, cut a piece from map ½" smaller on all sides than front cover. Apply spray adhesive to wrong side of map; center map on front cover and press firmly to secure.
2. For fabric trim, cut two ⅝"w strips ½" longer than length of map; cut two ⅝"w strips ½" longer than width of map. Referring to photo, cut corners of trim diagonally at a 45 degree angle. With corners meeting, glue trim to front of book, covering edge of map. Allow to dry.
3. Referring to photo, glue braid to fabric, turning at corners as shown in **Fig. 1**; trim excess braid.

Fig. 1

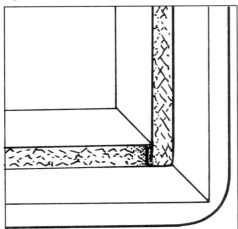

WOODEN PLACE MATS

These unique wooden place mats have a fresh country look. Stenciled with clusters of grapes and leafy grapevines, the pretty mats are easy to make in sets of two or more for holiday gifts.

For each place mat, you will need one 12" x 18" piece of ¼" A-2 birch veneer plywood, fine sandpaper, tack cloth, tracing paper, permanent felt-tip pen with fine point, purple and green acrylic paint, two 8½" x 11" sheets of acetate (available at craft or art supply stores), craft knife, cutting mat or a thick layer of newspapers, paper towels, removable tape (optional), small stencil brushes, wood stain, foam brushes, satin-finish clear polyurethane, one 11½" x 17½" piece of ¼" cork, and spray adhesive.

1. Sand plywood lightly until smooth. Remove dust with tack cloth.
2. Use stencil design, page 94, and follow **Transferring Patterns**, page 156.
3. Center 1 sheet of acetate over pattern and use pen to trace the outlines of all green areas. For placement guidelines, outline purple areas using dashed lines. Using remaining sheet of acetate, repeat for purple areas on pattern.

4. Place each acetate piece on cutting mat and use craft knife to cut out stencils along solid lines only, making sure edges are smooth.
5. Referring to photo, center leaf stencil ⅜" from 1 short edge of plywood. Hold or tape stencil in place while stenciling. Use a clean dry stencil brush for each color of paint. Dip brush in paint and remove excess on paper towel. Brush should be almost dry to produce a good design. Apply paint in a stamping motion. Allow to dry slightly; remove stencil. Repeat for remaining short edge.
6. Matching guidelines on grape stencil to previously stenciled areas, repeat Step 5 using remaining stencil
7. Following manufacturer's instructions, apply wood stain to top and sides of place mat; allow to dry.
8. Following manufacturer's instructions, apply 1 coat of polyurethane to place mat; allow to dry.

9. If desired, sand lightly and remove dust with tack cloth. Apply a second coat of polyurethane to place mat; allow to dry.
10. Spray back of place mat with adhesive. Center cork on back of place mat; allow to dry.

FOR LITTLE GIRLS

Inspired by the popular conversation hearts candy, these colorful accessories are fun and easy to make. Dainty painted hearts, pony beads, and ribbons lend fun and frills to our bracelet, barrette, socks, and shoes. They'll make any little girl happy!

BRACELET

You will need two 10½" lengths of ⅞"w grosgrain ribbon; thread to match grosgrain ribbon; 7" of ¾"w elastic; eight 5" lengths of ⅛"w satin ribbon; eight ¾"w wooden heart cutouts; lavender, pink, green, peach, and yellow acrylic paint; red permanent felt-tip pen with fine point; small round paintbrush; matte clear acrylic spray; fabric glue; hot glue gun; and glue sticks.

1. Matching edges, place ⅞" wide ribbon lengths together. Stitching close to edges, sew long edges together to form a casing.
2. Thread elastic through casing and secure at each end of casing with pins. Matching ends of casing, use a ¼" seam allowance to sew ends together. Finger press seam to 1 side and whipstitch in place. Turn bracelet right side out.
3. Paint heart cutouts desired colors; allow to dry. Spray cutouts with acrylic spray; allow to dry.
4. Use pen to write a message on each cutout (we wrote "HUG ME," "BE MINE," "CUTIE PIE," "MY LOVE," and "U R NICE").
5. Refer to photo and hot glue cutouts to bracelet. Tie satin ribbon lengths into bows; hot glue bows to bracelet. Place a small drop of fabric glue on knot of each bow to secure knot.

HAIR BOW

You will need 1⅓ yds each of ⅜"w and ⅝"w grosgrain ribbon for bow, five 18" lengths of ⅜"w grosgrain ribbon for curled ribbon, size 7 metal knitting needles or ¼" dia. wooden dowels, 32-gauge spool wire, spring-type clothespins, fabric glue, heart-shaped pony beads, hot glue gun, glue sticks, and ponytail barrette.

1. Center 1⅓ yd length of ⅜" wide ribbon on top of ⅝" wide ribbon. Beginning at 1 end of barrette and leaving 3" of ribbon extending past end of barrette, layer ribbons on barrette. Wrap wire tightly around ribbons and barrette several times, but do not cut wire (**Fig. 1**).

Fig. 1

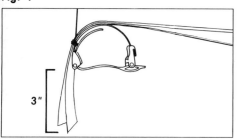

2. Make a 1¾" loop with layered ribbons; secure with wire (**Fig. 2**). Continue forming loops the length of barrette, leaving approximately 3" of ribbons extending at end of barrette. Cut off excess wire. Pull loops of ribbon apart for fullness.

Fig. 2

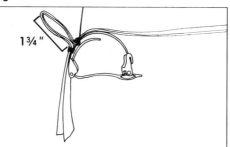

3. For curled ribbon, wet ribbon lengths. Overlapping long edges, tightly wrap 1 ribbon length around a knitting needle. Secure ribbon on knitting needle with clothespins. Repeat for remaining needle. Place needles on a baking sheet and dry in a preheated 250 degree oven for approximately 20 minutes or until dry. Repeat for remaining lengths.
4. Cut each curled ribbon into 3 equal lengths.
5. Refer to photo and hot glue 1 end of each curled ribbon length to base of bow.
6. Referring to photo, thread a bead onto each curled ribbon. Secure beads with dots of fabric glue.

SOCKS

You will need a pair of lace-trimmed ankle socks, two 1"w wooden heart cutouts, lavender and yellow acrylic paint, matte clear acrylic spray, four ⅔ yd lengths of desired color ⅛"w satin ribbon, small round paintbrush, washable fabric glue, two ½" dia. VELCRO® brand fasteners, and red permanent felt-tip pen with fine point.

1. Follow Steps 3 and 4 of Bracelet instructions to paint cutouts.
2. Cut ribbon lengths in half. Place half of ribbon lengths together; tie into a bow. Repeat for remaining lengths.
3. Glue 1 cutout to each bow. Glue hook side of 1 fastener to back of each bow; allow to dry.
4. Glue loop side of fastener to each sock cuff; allow to dry. Secure bow to sock.

SHOES

You will need a pair of white canvas tennis shoes; tracing paper; lavender, green, pink, peach, and yellow acrylic paint; two 1 yd lengths of ⅜"w grosgrain ribbon; 12 heart-shaped pony beads; ¾"w pregathered lace; small round paintbrush; red permanent felt-tip pen with fine point; and washable fabric glue.

1. Referring to **Fig. 3**, glue straight edge of lace inside edge of 1 shoe; trim excess lace. Allow to dry. Repeat for remaining shoe.

Fig. 3

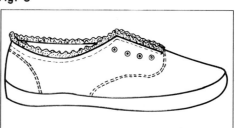

2. Trace heart pattern onto tracing paper and cut out.
3. To transfer heart design to shoes, refer to photo and place pattern on shoe; use a pencil to lightly draw around pattern. Repeat as desired.
4. Paint hearts desired colors; allow to dry.
5. Follow Step 4 of Bracelet instructions to write messages on each heart.
6. Lace shoes with ribbon lengths. Refer to photo and thread 3 beads onto each ribbon end; knot to secure.

RICH WRAP

Our beautiful border transforms a pretty but plain stadium blanket into a gift to be treasured. The stencil-inspired fruit design is cross-stitched on black fabric that is then sewn onto the afghan, adding a rich touch. Your friends will truly appreciate this lovely wrap!

You will need a stadium blanket (we used a 50" x 60" woven acrylic blanket), Black Aida (14 ct) (see Step 2 for amount), embroidery floss (see color key), embroidery hoop (optional), fabric for trim (see Step 5 for amount), and thread to match blanket and fabrics.

1. Trim fringe from blanket. Press raw edges ½" to wrong side; press ½" to wrong side again and hem.
2. Measure width of blanket and add 2". Cut a piece of Aida 10" wide by the determined measurement.
3. Center and stitch design on Aida. Repeat as necessary to within 2½" of each short edge, completing partial figures at each end. Use 3 strands of floss for Cross Stitch.
4. Trim long edges of Aida 1¼" from design.

5. Cut 2 strips from trim fabric 1" wide and the same length as Aida (pieced as necessary). Matching wrong sides and raw edges, press 1 trim strip in half lengthwise. Matching right sides and raw edges, use a ¼" seam allowance to sew trim strip to 1 long edge of Aida. Repeat to sew remaining trim strip to remaining long edge of Aida. Press

seam allowances toward Aida. Press short edges of border 1" to wrong side.
6. With bottom edge of border 2¾" from 1 short edge of blanket, pin border to right side of blanket. To sew border to blanket, machine stitch along each trim close to seamline. Whipstitch short edges of border to blanket.

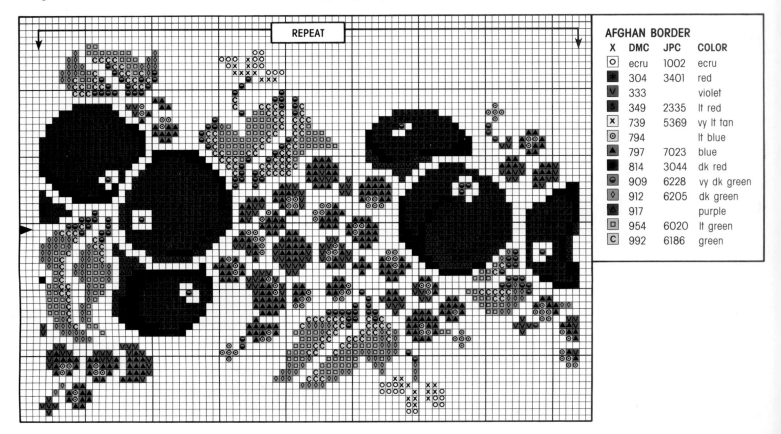

REPEAT

AFGHAN BORDER			
X	DMC	JPC	COLOR
○	ecru	1002	ecru
✳	304	3401	red
V	333		violet
s	349	2335	lt red
x	739	5369	vy lt tan
⊙	794		lt blue
▲	797	7023	blue
■	814	3044	dk red
⊖	909	6228	vy dk green
◊	912	6205	dk green
◣	917		purple
□	954	6020	lt green
C	992	6186	green

A WARMING GIFT

Wrapped in this pretty scarf, a favorite relative or friend is sure to have warm thoughts of you all winter long. The striking zigzag pattern, knitted in shades of berry red and peacock blue, is created with a combination of stockinette, cable, and slip stitches.

Finished Size: approximately 7" x 60"

ABBREVIATIONS

K   knit
P   purl
st(s) stitch(es)
C3L   cable 3 left
C3R   cable 3 right
MC   Main Color
CC   Contrasting Color

( ) — work enclosed instructions as many times as specified by the number immediately following **or** contains explanatory remarks.

MATERIALS

Bulky Weight Yarn, approximately:
  MC (berry red) — 5 ounces,
    (140 grams, 224 yards)
  CC (peacock blue) — 3 ounces,
    (80 grams, 128 yards)
Straight knitting needles, size 9
  (5.5 mm) **or** size needed for gauge
Cable needle
Yarn bobbin

GAUGE: In Stockinette Stitch,
    16 sts and 21 rows = 4"
    DO NOT HESITATE TO CHANGE
    NEEDLE SIZE TO OBTAIN
    CORRECT GAUGE.

PATTERN STITCHES

CABLE 3 LEFT (abbreviated C3L): Slip next st onto cable needle and hold at front of work, knit next 2 sts from left needle, then knit st from cable needle.
CABLE 3 RIGHT (abbreviated C3R): Slip next 2 sts onto cable needle and hold at back of work, knit next st from left needle, then knit sts from cable needle.

INSTRUCTIONS

Note: Wind 1 bobbin of MC. When changing colors, always pick up new color from beneath the dropped yarn and keep color just worked to the left.

With MC cast on 33 sts **loosely.**
Rows 1-6: Work in K1, P1 ribbing.
Row 7 (right side): (K1, P1) twice, with CC K 25, with MC on bobbin (P1, K1) twice.
Row 8: (P1, K1) twice, with CC P 25, with MC (K1, P1) twice.
Row 9: (K1, P1) twice, K 5, (slip 1 as if to **knit**, K 3) 5 times, (P1, K1) twice.
Row 10: (P1, K1) twice, (P 3, slip 1 as if to **knit**) 5 times, P 5, (K1, P1) twice.
Row 11: (K1, P1) twice, with CC K 3,

(C3R, K1) 5 times, K2, with MC (P1, K1) twice.
Row 12: (P1, K1) twice, with CC P 25, with MC (K1, P1) twice.
Row 13: (K1, P1) twice, K1, (slip 1 as if to **purl**, K 3) 6 times, (P1, K1) twice.
Row 14: (P1, K1) twice, (P 3, slip 1 as if to **purl**) 6 times, P1, (K1, P1) twice.
Row 15: (K1, P1) twice, with CC K1, (C3L, K1) 6 times, with MC (P1, K1) twice.
Repeat Rows 8-15 until scarf measures approximately 59" from cast on edge, ending by working Row 12.
Repeat Rows 1-6.
Bind off all sts **loosely** in ribbing. Weave in all ends.

BABY'S FIRST NOEL

With this precious set, baby can enjoy Christmas dinner in holiday style. The terry-lined bib features shiny jingle bells and a candy-striped binding. Sized just for little ones, the matching place mat has a cross-stitched Ribband® trim to celebrate baby's first Noel.

For place mat, you will need one 14" x 22" piece of fabric for place mat, one 1" x 36" bias strip of fabric (pieced as necessary) and 36" of ⅛" dia. cord for cording, one 3½" x 68" strip of fabric (pieced as necessary) for ruffle, 12" of Maxi Ribband® II, and embroidery floss (see color key).

For bib, you will need one 8" x 10" piece of fabric, one 8" x 10" piece of terry cloth, one 1½" x 50" bias strip of fabric (pieced as necessary) for binding and ties, heavy thread (buttonhole twist), and three ½" dia. jingle bells.

You will also need tracing paper and thread to match fabrics.

PLACE MAT

1. Work design on Ribband® using 2 strands of floss for Cross Stitch and 1 strand for French Knots.
2. For pattern, fold a 15" square of tracing paper in half from top to bottom and again from left to right. Place folds along dashed lines of pattern, page 101. Trace pattern. Cutting through all thicknesses of paper, cut out pattern. Use pattern and cut 2 pieces from place mat fabric.
3. Referring to **Fig. 1**, place Ribband® on right side of 1 place mat piece (top); baste in place. Trim ends of Ribband® even with edges of fabric.

Fig. 1

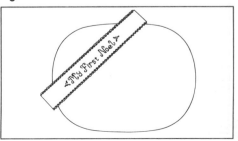

4. For cording, lay cord along center on wrong side of bias strip. Matching long edges, fold strip over cord. Use a zipper foot and machine baste along length of strip close to cord.

5. Matching raw edges and beginning 1" from end of cording, baste cording to right side of top fabric piece; clip seam allowance as needed. Open ends of cording and cut cord to fit exactly. Insert 1 end of cording fabric in the other; fold raw edge of top fabric ½" to wrong side and baste in place.

6. For ruffle, match right sides and short edges of ruffle fabric. Use a ½" seam allowance to sew short edges together to form a loop; press seam open. With wrong sides together, match raw edges and fold fabric in half; press. Baste ⅜" and ¼" from raw edges. Pull basting threads, drawing up gathers to fit place mat top. Matching raw edges, baste ruffle to right side of place mat top.

7. With place mat pieces right sides together and leaving an opening for turning, use a zipper foot and sew place mat pieces together as close as possible to cording. Clip seam allowance and turn right side out; press. Sew final closure by hand.

BIB

1. Use bib pattern and follow **Transferring Patterns**, page 156.

2. Use pattern and cut 1 piece from bib fabric and 1 piece from terry cloth. Matching wrong sides and raw edges, baste pieces together.

3. For binding, match wrong sides and raw edges and fold bias strip in half lengthwise; press. Fold long raw edges to center; press.

4. To bind top of bib, cut a 7" strip from binding. Referring to **Fig. 2**, insert top edge of bib between folded edges of binding; pin in place.

Fig. 2

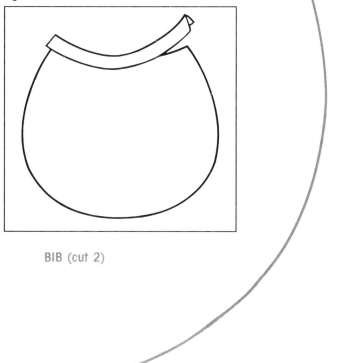

BIB (cut 2)

PLACE MAT (cut 2)

5. Stitch all layers together close to inner edge of binding. Trim ends of binding close to bib.

6. Open ends of remaining binding; press ends ¼" to wrong side. Refold binding.

7. Beginning 12" from 1 end of binding, insert side and bottom edges of bib between folded edges of binding; pin in place.

8. Beginning at 1 end of binding, stitch all layers together close to inner edge of binding; continue stitching to end of binding strip. Press.

9. Referring to photo, use heavy thread and securely sew jingle bells to center front of bib.

BABY'S FIRST NOEL (101w x 14h)	
Aida 11	9¼" x 1⅜"
Aida 14	7¼" x 1"
Aida 18	5⅝" x ⅞"
Hardanger 22	4⅝" x ¾"

BABY'S FIRST NOEL (101w x 14h)		
X	DMC	COLOR
▣	367	green
◉	890	dk green
•	321	red French Knot

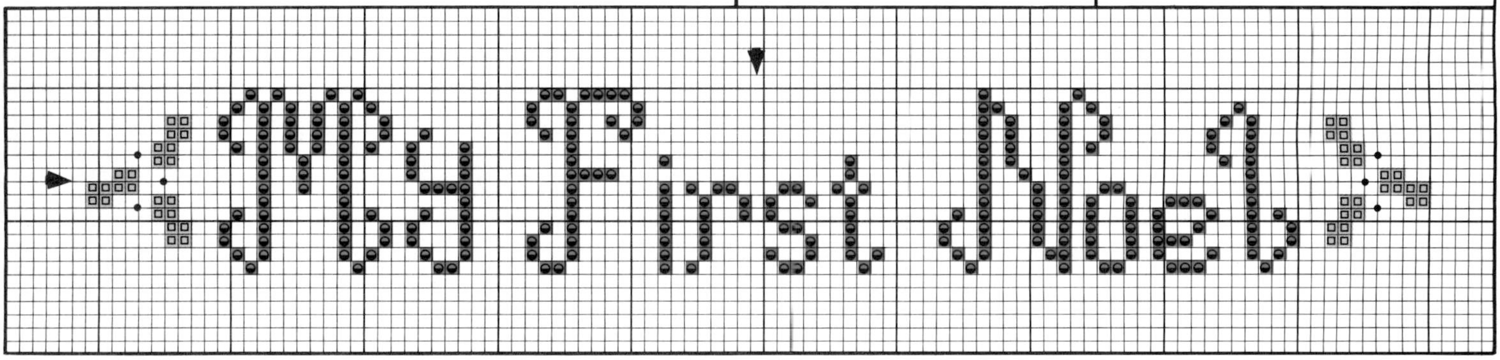

A TIMELY GIFT

This little clock makes a timely gift. Painted in simple folk art style and antiqued, the wooden clock features a sprinkling of stars against a background of deep blue. It's sure to delight anyone on your list.

You will need a 2⅜" x 6" x 7⅜" unpainted wooden clock (we used a Hastings Carriage Clock from Walnut Hollow Farm®), fine sandpaper, acrylic paint (see color key), Duncan Quik-Crackle™ crackling medium, black permanent felt-tip pen with extra-fine point, waterbase wood stain, matte waterbase varnish, battery-operated clock movement kit and black clock hands (available at craft stores), four ⅝" dia. black wooden beads, tack cloth, tracing paper, graphite transfer paper, 5" long black wrought iron drawer handle with screws, screwdriver, paintbrushes, and a soft cloth.

1. Sand clock lightly; remove dust with tack cloth.
2. Using dk brown paint for basecoat and cream paint for contrast, follow manufacturer's instructions to apply paint and crackling medium to clock; allow to dry.
3. Trace face pattern onto tracing paper.
4. Center pattern on clock front and use transfer paper to transfer design to clock.
5. Allowing paint to dry between colors, refer to photo and color key to paint clock. Use pen to draw over numbers and fine lines on dial.
6. Apply stain to clock; remove excess with soft cloth. Allow to dry.
7. Apply varnish to clock; allow to dry.
8. Attach handle to center top of clock.
9. Follow manufacturer's instructions to assemble and attach clock movement and hands.
10. With bead hole against clock bottom, glue each bead to bottom of clock at corners.

CLOCK FACE

Basecoat and heavy outlines — dk brown
Contrast — cream
Molding grooves — red
Background — blue
Stars and numbers — gold
Border around numbers — red

VILLAGE PLAY MAT

This fold-out village will provide hours of entertainment for small children! Appliquéd with colorful shapes and a winding road, it's great for playing with toy cars, farm animals, and more. The handy mat even has carrying straps so it can be folded up and taken along for a portable play area.

For mat, you will need one 36" x 38" piece of fabric for mat background, one 36" x 38" piece of fabric for backing, 2 yds of 1"w nylon strapping for handle, 3 yds of 22"w paper-backed fusible web, thread to match backing fabric and strapping, tracing paper, white acrylic paint, and small round paintbrush.

For appliqués, you will need ½ yd of 44"w black fabric, one 10" square of white fabric, one 10" square of red fabric, one 5" square of brown fabric, one 10" square of lt green fabric, one 10" x 20" piece of dk green fabric, one 7" square of purple fabric, one 12" square of blue fabric, and one 7" square of yellow fabric.

1. Wash, dry, and press all fabrics.
2. Use patterns, pages 105 and 106, and follow **Transferring Patterns**, page 156.

3. Cut a piece of web slightly smaller than each appliqué fabric piece. Follow manufacturer's instructions to fuse web to wrong sides of fabric pieces.
4. Use patterns and cut shapes from appliqué fabrics. Referring to Diagram, page 105, and photo, position shapes on background fabric; fuse in place.
5. Referring to photo, paint approximately ½" long stripes spaced ½" apart along center of road.
6. Cut web 1" smaller than backing fabric (web may be pieced as necessary). Follow manufacturer's instructions to fuse web to center of wrong side of backing fabric. Remove paper backing.
7. For handle, match right sides and raw edges and use a ½" seam allowance to sew ends of strapping together; finger press seam open. Refer to **Fig. 1** to place strapping on right side

of backing fabric. Sew strapping to fabric where indicated by dashed lines in **Fig. 1**.

Fig. 1

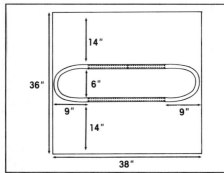

8. Matching right sides and raw edges and leaving an opening for turning, use a ½" seam allowance to sew mat and backing together. Cut corners diagonally and trim seam allowance; turn right side out. Sew final closure by hand.

9. Place mat on flat surface and follow manufacturer's instructions to fuse mat and backing together.

10. To fold mat for carrying, fold lengthwise into thirds; fold ends toward center.

DIAGRAM

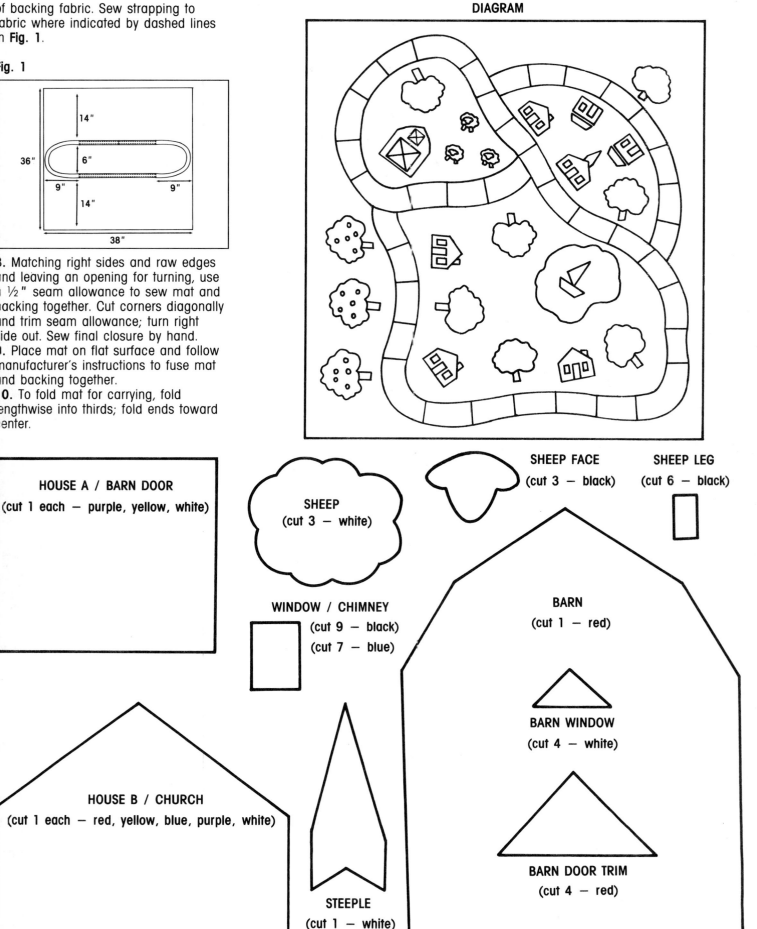

HOUSE A / BARN DOOR
(cut 1 each — purple, yellow, white)

SHEEP
(cut 3 — white)

WINDOW / CHIMNEY
(cut 9 — black)
(cut 7 — blue)

SHEEP FACE
(cut 3 — black)

SHEEP LEG
(cut 6 — black)

BARN
(cut 1 — red)

BARN WINDOW
(cut 4 — white)

BARN DOOR TRIM
(cut 4 — red)

HOUSE B / CHURCH
(cut 1 each — red, yellow, blue, purple, white)

STEEPLE
(cut 1 — white)

Continued on page 106

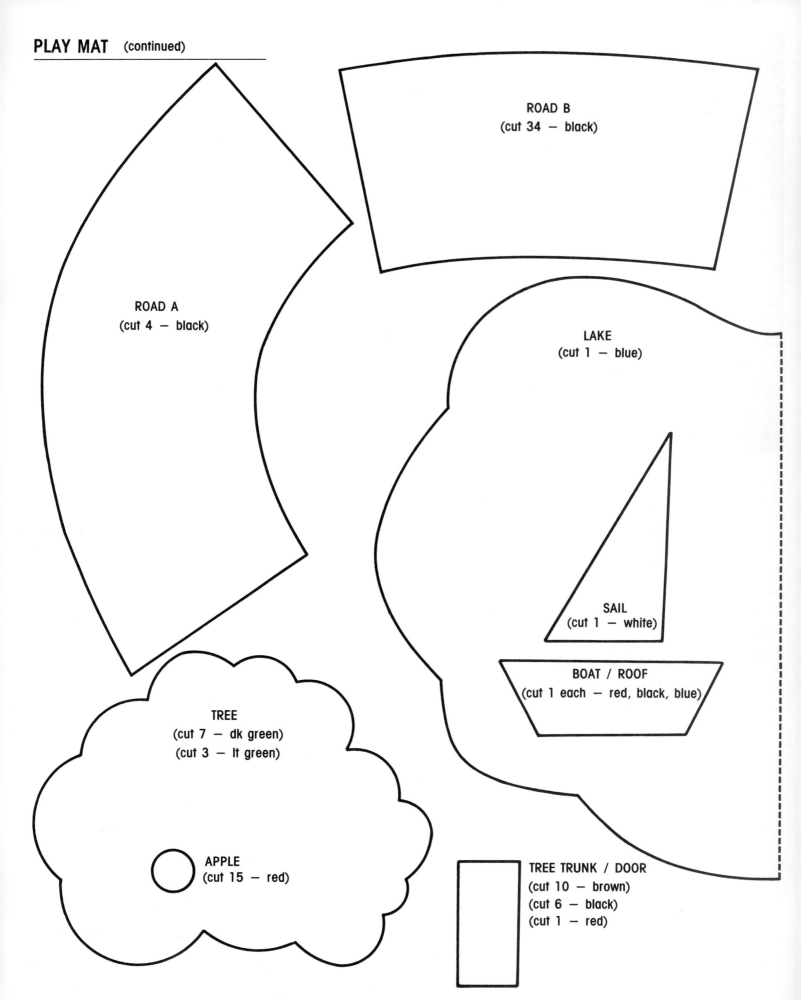

ROAD B
(cut 34 — black)

ROAD A
(cut 4 — black)

LAKE
(cut 1 — blue)

SAIL
(cut 1 — white)

BOAT / ROOF
(cut 1 each — red, black, blue)

TREE
(cut 7 — dk green)
(cut 3 — lt green)

APPLE
(cut 15 — red)

TREE TRUNK / DOOR
(cut 10 — brown)
(cut 6 — black)
(cut 1 — red)

POTPOURRI COTTAGE

Inspired by Victorian-style gingerbread houses, this quaint cottage smells as sweet as it looks — the roof lifts off to reveal a secret cache of holiday potpourri. The little house is created in plastic canvas needlepoint using fabric strips instead of yarn. It's a charming way to share the scents of the season!

You will need three 10½" x 13½" sheets of 7 mesh plastic canvas, 44"w print or solid color cotton fabrics (refer to color key, page 108, for colors and amounts), #16 tapestry needle, craft glue, and potpourri.

1. Wash, dry, and press all fabrics; cut off selvages. Tear fabrics into ¼" x 44" strips.
2. (**Note:** To cut plastic canvas pieces accurately, count threads, not holes.) Follow charts, pages 108 and 109, to cut out plastic canvas pieces.
3. (**Note:** Use fabric strips to stitch house. Tent Stitch, Gobelin Stitch, Backstitch, French Knot, and Overcast Stitch are used. Stitch Diagrams are on pages 156 and 157.) Follow charts and use required stitches to work house pieces.
4. (**Note:** Refer to photo to assemble house. Use brown for joining in Steps 4 – 6.) Matching ✱'s and ☐'s,

join Shutters to Front, Back, and Sides between ✱'s and ☐'s.
5. With right sides out and matching ▲'s and ★'s, join Sides to Front and Back along lt brown areas of Sides, Front, and Back.
6. Join Front to Base between △'s. Repeat to join Back to Base.
7. (**Note:** Use white for joining in Steps 7 – 13.) Join remaining unworked side edges of Sides to Front and Back. Join remaining unworked edges of Front, Back, and Sides to Base.
8. With wrong sides facing and matching ♦'s, join Gables between ♦'s.
9. With wrong sides facing and matching ■'s, join Roof Front and Back between ■'s.
10. Matching ✚'s, tack Roof to Gables at ✚'s.
11. Beginning at top point and stitching toward each end of Front Roof Trim,

Continued on page 108

107

POTPOURRI COTTAGE (continued)

match ○'s and ☉'s and join Front Roof Trim to Gables and Roof between ○'s and ☉'s. Repeat to join Back Roof Trim to Gables and Roof.

12. Beginning at top point and stitching toward each end of Side Roof Trim, join Side Roof Trim to 1 side of Roof along unworked edges of Roof. Join Side Roof Trim to Front and Back Roof Trim along unworked edges. Repeat for remaining side of Roof.

13. With right sides out and matching ◓'s and ◆'s, join Chimney Sides to Chimney Front and Back between ◓'s and ◆'s. Join Chimney Cap Trim pieces along short edges. Join Chimney Cap Trim to Chimney Cap along unworked edges. Glue Chimney Cap over top of Chimney. Glue Chimney to Roof.

14. Fill house with potpourri and place roof on house.

╱	white — ½ yd
╱	gold — ¼ yd
╱	red — ½ yd
╱	green — ¼ yd
╱	lt brown — 1 yd
╱	brown — ¼ yd
●	red Fr. Knot

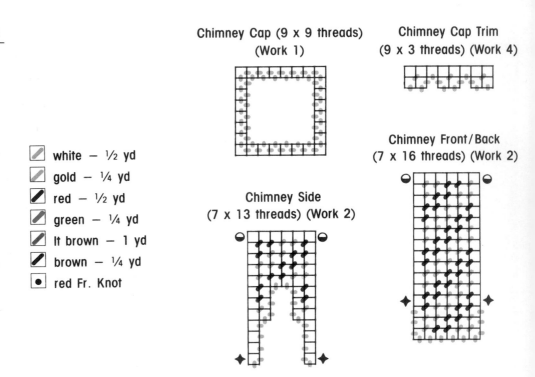

Chimney Cap (9 x 9 threads) (Work 1)

Chimney Cap Trim (9 x 3 threads) (Work 4)

Chimney Front/Back (7 x 16 threads) (Work 2)

Chimney Side (7 x 13 threads) (Work 2)

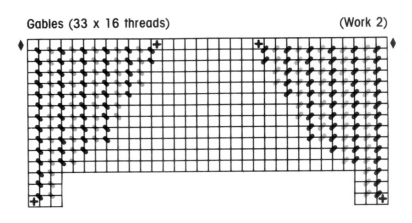

Gables (33 x 16 threads)　　　　(Work 2)

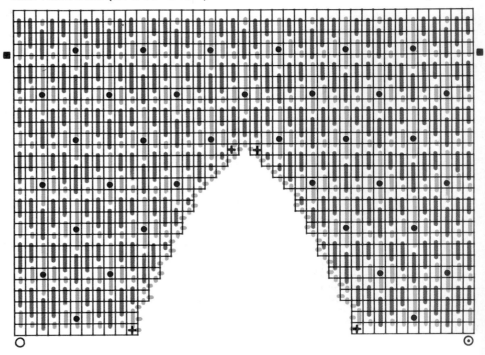

Roof Front/Back (42 x 30 threads)　　　　(Work 2)

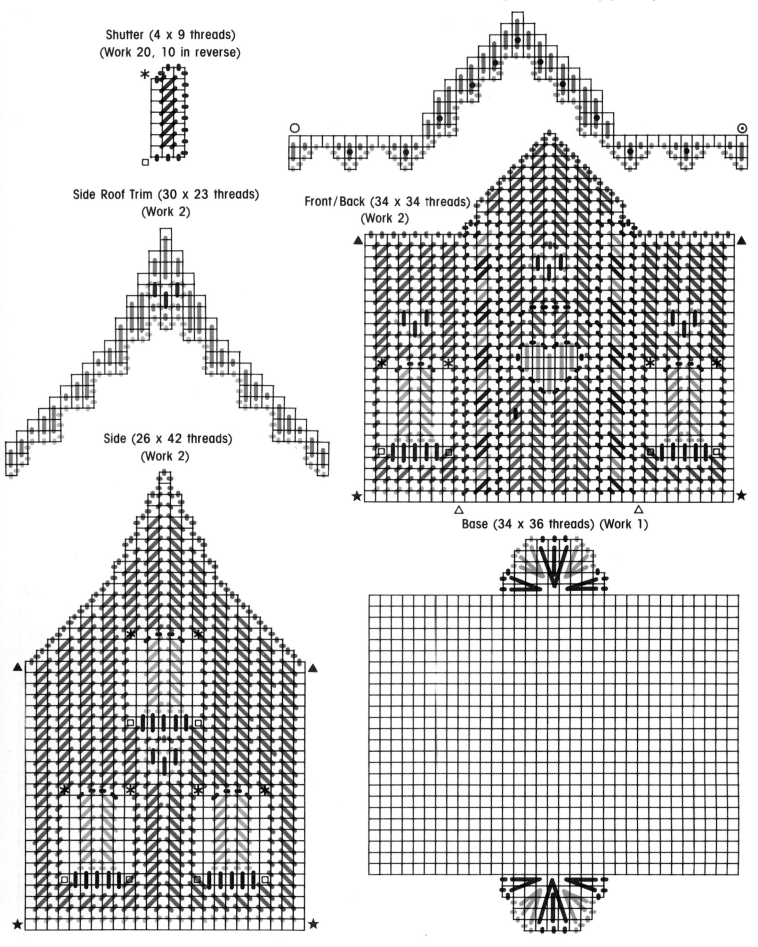

Shutter (4 x 9 threads)
(Work 20, 10 in reverse)

Front/Back Roof Trim (42 x 15 threads) (Work 2)

Side Roof Trim (30 x 23 threads)
(Work 2)

Front/Back (34 x 34 threads)
(Work 2)

Side (26 x 42 threads)
(Work 2)

Base (34 x 36 threads) (Work 1)

THE TASTES OF CHRISTMAS

Christmas has ever been the season of feasting and merrymaking. Touched by its jovial mood, we turn to our kitchens to create delicious holiday fare. From there we send out season's greetings in gaily wrapped packages of Christmas treats. Filled with the spirit of hospitality, we also prepare splendid banquets and set our tables with fine linens, elegant china, and gleaming silver in honor of the gala occasion. What joy we find as we welcome family and friends to the Yuletide celebration!

Christmas Eve Dinner

*Planning a wonderful menu is the first step in hosting an unforgettable holiday meal.
Whether you serve one of our two complete menus or combine dishes from both,
your Christmas Eve dinner is sure to be extra special this year.*

Shrimp Mousse	Smoked Parmesan Almonds
Frozen Strawberry Salad	Lobster Bisque
Cider-Baked Ham	Tenderloin of Beef in Pastry
Red and Green Vegetable Medley	Creamy Pesto Spinach
Corn Bread Loaf	Onion Casserole
Peachy Sweet Potatoes	Festive Rice Cups
Flaming Bread Pudding	Raspberry Soufflé

This Tenderloin of Beef in Pastry showcases a succulent beef fillet with mushrooms and green onions.

TENDERLOIN OF BEEF IN PASTRY

- 3 to 4 pound beef tenderloin, trimmed of fat
- 1 teaspoon salt, divided
- 1 teaspoon ground black pepper, divided
- ½ cup butter or margarine
- 1 pound fresh mushrooms, chopped
- 4 green onions, finely chopped
- 1 sheet frozen puff pastry, thawed
- 1 egg yolk
- 1 teaspoon water

Preheat oven to 400 degrees. Rub beef with ½ teaspoon salt and ½ teaspoon pepper. Cook beef in roasting pan 25 to 30 minutes or until a meat thermometer inserted in center of meat registers 120 degrees. Cool to room temperature. Reduce oven temperature to 350 degrees.

In a medium skillet, melt butter over medium-high heat. Stir in mushrooms, onions, and remaining salt and pepper. Sauté 2 to 3 minutes or until onions are soft.

On a lightly floured surface, use a floured rolling pin to roll out pastry to a 10 x 13-inch rectangle (or large enough to wrap completely around beef). Mix egg yolk and water in a small bowl. Spread mushroom mixture evenly on rolled pastry to within 2 inches of each edge. Center beef on pastry. Fold pastry around beef and seal edges with egg yolk. Place beef, seam side down, on a greased baking sheet. Brush top of pastry with egg yolk. Using dough scraps or another sheet of pastry, cut shapes from dough for garnish. Arrange cutouts on top of pastry; brush with remaining egg yolk. Bake 25 to 30 minutes or until meat thermometer registers 130 degrees. If pastry browns too quickly, cover with aluminum foil. Cool 10 minutes. Slice to serve.
Yield: about 10 servings

Chopped celery adds crunch to cool, refreshing Shrimp Mousse. We garnished it with fresh avocado slices and crispy crackers for serving.

SHRIMP MOUSSE

- 12 ounces frozen cooked shrimp (about 2 cups), thawed and finely chopped
- ½ cup finely chopped celery
- 3 tablespoons lemon juice
- 2 tablespoons white wine vinegar
- 1 teaspoon prepared horseradish
- 1 teaspoon ground black pepper
- ½ teaspoon salt
- 1 envelope unflavored gelctin
- ¼ cup water
- ½ cup whipping cream
- 4 ounces (½ of 8-ounce package) cream cheese, softened
- ⅓ cup mayonnaise

Avocado slices and crackers to serve

To marinate shrimp, combine first 7 ingredients in a large bowl. Cover and refrigerate 8 hours or overnight. In a small saucepan, combine gelatin and water over low heat, stirring until gelatin is dissolved. Remove from heat; cool to room temperature. In a large bowl, whip cream until stiff. Stir in gelatin, cream cheese, mayonnaise, and shrimp mixture. Pour into a greased 8-inch diameter ring mold. Chill 4 to 5 hours, stirring occasionally until mixture begins to set. To unmold, dip mold into hot water up to rim and invert onto a serving plate. Serve with avocado slices and crackers.
Yield: 10 to 12 servings

LOBSTER BISQUE

- 1 gallon water
- 4 lobster tails (about 4 pounds)
- 6 tablespoons butter or margarine, divided
- ⅓ cup cognac
- ½ cup plus 3 tablespoons chopped green onions, divided
- 4 cloves garlic, minced
- 3 tablespoons tomato paste
- 2½ cups dry white wine
- 1 teaspoon dried tarragon
- ½ teaspoon dried thyme
- ¼ teaspoon ground cayenne pepper
- 2 bay leaves
- 3 tablespoons all-purpose flour
- 2½ cups milk
- ¾ cup cream
- 1 teaspoon salt
- ¼ teaspoon ground black pepper
- 2 egg yolks

  Cream to garnish

In a Dutch oven, heat water to boiling. Add lobster, cover, and cook about 12 minutes or until lobster is pink. Remove lobster from water and cool to room temperature. Reserve 4 cups of water used for cooking. Remove lobster meat from shells and finely dice.

For stock, melt 3 tablespoons butter in Dutch oven over medium heat. Stir in cognac. Bring mixture to a boil and simmer 3 minutes. Stir in reserved water, ½ cup green onions, and next 7 ingredients. Simmer 30 minutes longer. Strain into a large bowl.

In Dutch oven, melt remaining butter over medium-high heat. Add remaining green onions and sauté 2 minutes. Whisk flour into butter mixture and cook 1 minute longer, stirring constantly. Whisk in stock and next 5 ingredients until blended. Bring to a boil, reduce heat to medium-low, and simmer 5 minutes. Stir in lobster meat. Simmer 10 to 15 minutes longer or until heated through. Garnish each serving with about 1 tablespoon cream and swirl with a knife. Serve immediately.

Yield: about 8 servings

Perfect for nibbling before dinner, Smoked Parmesan Almonds have a crispy cheese coating. The creamy Lobster Bisque is flavored with a hint of cognac and elegantly garnished with a swirl of cream.

SMOKED PARMESAN ALMONDS

- 1 large egg white
- 1 cup whole unsalted almonds
- 2 tablespoons butter or margarine
- 2 teaspoons liquid smoke flavoring
- 1 teaspoon salt
- ¼ cup Parmesan cheese

Preheat oven to 350 degrees. In a small bowl, beat egg white until foamy. Stir in almonds, coating well.

In a small saucepan, melt butter over medium heat. Stir in remaining ingredients. Add almonds to butter mixture, stirring until well coated. Pour onto an ungreased baking sheet. Bake 25 to 30 minutes or until cheese is brown. Cool completely on pan. Store in an airtight container.

Yield: about 1 cup nuts

Basted and browned to perfection, juicy Cider-Baked Ham is served with a tangy-sweet sauce. Slices of sage-flavored Corn Bread Loaf are a tasty variation of traditional dressing.

CIDER-BAKED HAM

    5 to 6 pound ham
    2 cups apple cider, divided
 ¼ cup soy sauce
    2 tablespoons cornstarch
    1 tablespoon water

Preheat oven to 450 degrees. Place ham in a large roasting pan. Bake 30 minutes or until outside is crisp. Remove from oven. Reduce oven temperature to 325 degrees.

In a large bowl, combine 1½ cups cider and soy sauce; pour over ham. Cover and bake 2 to 3 hours or until meat thermometer registers 185 degrees, basting ham frequently with cider mixture.

For sauce, combine meat drippings and remaining cider in a medium saucepan. In a small bowl, mix together cornstarch and water to make a paste.

Spoon into meat drippings, stirring until smooth. Cook over medium heat 10 to 15 minutes or until thick, stirring occasionally. Transfer ham to serving plate and serve with sauce.
Yield: 12 to 16 servings

CORN BREAD LOAF

    6 tablespoons butter or margarine
    1 cup chopped green onions
 ¾ cup chopped celery
    4 cups corn bread crumbs
    4 cups fine plain bread crumbs
 10 slices bacon, cooked and
       crumbled
 1½ teaspoons ground sage
 ¾ teaspoon salt
 ½ teaspoon ground black pepper

    6 eggs, beaten
    1 cup chicken broth

Preheat oven to 350 degrees. In a large skillet, melt butter over medium-high heat. Stir in onions and celery and sauté 8 minutes or until soft. In a large bowl, combine corn bread crumbs and bread crumbs. Stir in onion mixture and next 4 ingredients. Stir in eggs and chicken broth. Spoon evenly into a greased and floured 4 x 12-inch loaf pan. Bake 30 to 40 minutes or until top is brown. Unmold onto serving plate and slice. Serve immediately.
Yield: about 10 servings

This savory Onion Casserole combines red, yellow, and green onions in a sauce of Havarti and bleu cheeses with white wine.

ONION CASSEROLE

2 large yellow onions, thinly sliced and separated into rings, divided
2 large red onions, thinly sliced and separated into rings, divided
12 green onions, chopped, divided
1 teaspoon ground black pepper, divided
10 ounces bleu cheese, crumbled
10 ounces (about 2½ cups) grated Havarti cheese
3 tablespoons butter or margarine, cut into small pieces
¾ cup dry white wine

Preheat oven to 350 degrees. In a greased 9 x 13-inch baking dish, layer one-half of yellow, red, and green onions. Sprinkle ½ teaspoon pepper over onions. Top with bleu cheese. Layer remaining onions and sprinkle remaining pepper over top. Top with Havarti cheese. Place butter evenly over cheese. Pour wine over casserole. Bake 1 hour or until onions are tender. If cheese browns too quickly, cover with aluminum foil. Serve hot.
Yield: about 12 servings
Note: Casserole may be assembled 1 day in advance and refrigerated. If refrigerated, increase baking time to 1 hour 15 minutes.

FROZEN STRAWBERRY SALAD

1 package (8 ounces) cream cheese, softened
⅓ cup sour cream
1 teaspoon lemon juice
3 tablespoons granulated sugar
½ cup whipping cream
3 cups sliced fresh strawberries
½ cup chopped pecans

In a large bowl, combine first 4 ingredients, beating until smooth. In another large bowl, whip cream until stiff. Fold whipped cream, strawberries, and pecans into cream cheese mixture. Pour into an 8 x 11-inch pan. Freeze 4 hours or until firm. Cut into 2½-inch squares. Serve immediately.
Yield: about 12 servings

Creamy Frozen Strawberry Salad features fresh strawberries and chopped pecans.

Broccoli and cherry tomatoes seasoned with lemon and basil make up the Red and Green Vegetable Medley *(left)*. Festive Rice Cups *(center)* are mildly flavored with onion and sweet peppers, and our recipe for Peachy Sweet Potatoes is an innovative version of a holiday favorite.

PEACHY SWEET POTATOES

    2 large sweet potatoes, peeled and
        cut into pieces
    6 cups water
    2 tablespoons firmly packed brown
        sugar
    ¼ teaspoon salt
    ¼ teaspoon ground cloves
    1 teaspoon lemon juice
    2 tablespoons butter or margarine,
        softened
    2 cans (29 ounces each) peach
        halves, drained

In a large saucepan, cook potatoes in boiling water 25 to 30 minutes or until tender; drain. Cool to room temperature. In a large bowl, mash potatoes. Mix in next 5 ingredients, beating until smooth.

Preheat oven to 400 degrees. Place peach halves in an ungreased 9 x 13-inch baking pan. Using a pastry bag fitted with a large star tip, pipe potato mixture into center of each peach half. Bake 15 minutes or until potato mixture is light brown. Serve immediately.
Yield: 12 to 14 servings

FESTIVE RICE CUPS

    3 tablespoons butter or margarine
    3 tablespoons olive oil
    1 cup chopped onion
    5 cups chicken broth
    2 cups uncooked brown rice
    ¼ teaspoon ground turmeric
    ½ teaspoon salt
    ¼ teaspoon ground black pepper
    ¼ cup chopped green pepper
    ¼ cup chopped red pepper

In a large saucepan, melt butter with oil over medium-high heat. Add onion and sauté until golden brown. Add next 5 ingredients. Bring to a boil and reduce heat to low. Cover and simmer 50 to 60 minutes or until all liquid is absorbed. Stir in red and green peppers. For each serving, firmly press about ½ cup rice into a 3-inch tart mold; invert onto plate. Serve immediately.
Yield: 8 to 10 servings

RED AND GREEN VEGETABLE MEDLEY

    1 large bunch fresh broccoli,
        cleaned and chopped
    ¾ cup water
    ¼ cup butter or margarine
    3 tablespoons lemon juice
    ½ teaspoon ground dried basil
    ½ teaspoon salt
    ¼ teaspoon ground black pepper
    1 pint cherry tomatoes, halved

In a large saucepan, cook broccoli in water until tender. Rinse with cold water and drain well. In a large skillet, melt butter over medium-high heat. Stir in broccoli and next 4 ingredients. Cook over high heat 1 to 2 minutes, stirring constantly. Add tomatoes and toss. Serve immediately.
Yield: about 6 servings

RASPBERRY SOUFFLÉ

SOUFFLÉ

- 8 eggs, separated
- 1 cup granulated sugar
- 1 cup puréed raspberries
- ¼ cup crème de cassis liqueur
- 2 envelopes unflavored gelatin
- ½ cup lemon juice
- 2 cups whipping cream

SAUCE

- 2 cups sliced fresh or frozen strawberries
- ½ cup granulated sugar
- 4 tablespoons orange-flavored liqueur

For soufflé, prepare a 2-quart soufflé dish with a waxed paper collar extending 2 to 3 inches above rim of dish. Tape in place. Grease dish, including collar. In a medium bowl, beat egg yolks and sugar until fluffy. Stir in raspberries and crème de cassis. In a medium saucepan, combine gelatin and lemon juice over low heat, stirring until gelatin is dissolved. Stir raspberry mixture into gelatin, mixing well. Cook over medium-low heat until mixture coats the back of a spoon (about 5 minutes). Cool to room temperature.

In a large bowl, beat egg whites until stiff. In a chilled large bowl, whip cream until stiff. Fold egg whites into raspberry mixture. Gently fold in whipped cream. Pour into soufflé dish and chill 8 hours or overnight. Remove paper collar before serving.

For sauce, combine strawberries and sugar in a medium saucepan over medium heat. Cook 2 to 3 minutes or until heated through. Remove from heat and stir in liqueur. Serve with soufflé.
Yield: 8 to 10 servings

A spirited sauce of strawberries and orange liqueur complements this elegant Raspberry Soufflé.

CREAMY PESTO SPINACH

- 3 medium tomatoes
- 1 tablespoon salt
- 2 packages (10 ounces each) frozen chopped spinach, thawed and squeezed dry
- ¼ cup prepared pesto sauce
- ½ cup whipping cream
- ⅔ cup grated Romano cheese
- 1 teaspoon ground black pepper
- 1 tablespoon grated Parmesan cheese

Cut tomatoes in half; remove seeds and pulp. Sprinkle salt inside tomato shells and turn upside down on a wire rack to drain 30 minutes. Use a paper towel to pat inside of each tomato dry.

Preheat oven to 400 degrees. In a medium skillet, cook spinach over medium heat 5 to 10 minutes or until heated through. Stir in pesto sauce; cook 2 to 3 minutes longer. Stir in cream; cook until mixture is thick (about 2 minutes). Stir in Romano cheese and pepper. Spoon about ½ cup spinach into each tomato shell. Sprinkle Parmesan cheese over top. Bake in a greased 8-inch square baking pan 10 minutes or until heated through. Serve immediately.
Yield: 6 servings

Creamy Pesto Spinach is presented in tomato cups to create a festive color combination.

FLAMING BREAD PUDDING

PUDDING

    2 cups raisins
    1 cup cooking sherry
    1 cup butter or margarine, softened
    1 cup granulated sugar
    1 cup all-purpose flour
    1 teaspoon baking soda
    ½ teaspoon salt
    4 eggs, beaten
    2 cups finely chopped dates
    1½ cups grated carrots
    1½ cups chopped pecans
    1 cup fine plain bread crumbs
    1 cup milk
    ¼ cup molasses
    1 tablespoon dried orange peel
    1 tablespoon dried lemon peel
    2 teaspoons ground cinnamon
    ½ teaspoon ground cloves
    ½ teaspoon ground nutmeg
    ¼ teaspoon ground mace
    ¼ cup cognac

SAUCE

    3 eggs, separated
    1 cup granulated sugar
    2 tablespoons butter or margarine,
        softened
    1 cup whipping cream, whipped
        until stiff
    3 tablespoons brandy

    ¼ cup cognac

For pudding, soak raisins in sherry 8 hours or overnight. In a large bowl, cream butter and sugar until fluffy. Blend in next 3 ingredients. Stir in raisins (including sherry) and remaining pudding ingredients, mixing well. Spoon into a greased 3-quart metal mold with lid. Cover loosely with lid. Place mold on a wire rack in the bottom of a large stock pot. Fill pot with boiling water to reach halfway up sides of mold. Cover pot and steam pudding in simmering water over medium heat about 5 hours. Check water level occasionally; add hot water as needed. Remove mold from water, uncover, and cool 30 minutes. Invert onto a serving plate, leaving pudding in mold until completely cooled.

For sauce, beat egg yolks in a large bowl. Add sugar and butter; beat until thick. In a large bowl, beat egg whites until stiff; fold into egg yolk mixture. Fold in whipped cream and brandy.

Heat cognac in a small saucepan over medium heat. Remove from heat and carefully ignite with a long kitchen match. Pour over pudding. When flames die, slice and serve with sauce.

Yield: 10 to 12 servings

Flaming Bread Pudding makes a grand finale to Christmas Eve dinner. Laden with fruits and nuts, the traditional steamed pudding is served with a creamy brandy sauce.

An Elegant Open House

At Christmastime, the spirit of the season inspires us to open our homes to friends and neighbors. An air of gracious hospitality fills the house, inviting guests to linger and enjoy an evening of yuletide cheer. Adding to the festive atmosphere, a choice selection of appetizers and beverages makes the occasion even more memorable. With this collection of elegant and delicious recipes, you can host an open house as lovely as ours.

Wreathed with broccoli flowerets and garnished with colorful peppers, this Fresh Vegetable Tart includes crunchy carrots, broccoli, and green onions in a creamy filling.

FRESH VEGETABLE TART

CRUST

- 1¼ cups all-purpose flour
- ¼ teaspoon salt
- 7 tablespoons butter or margarine, chilled and cut into pieces
- 3 tablespoons ice water

FILLING

- 12 ounces (one and one-half 8-ounce packages) cream cheese, softened
- 1 package (1 ounce) ranch salad dressing mix
- ¼ cup mayonnaise
- ⅓ cup sour cream
- ½ cup chopped fresh broccoli
- ½ cup chopped fresh carrot
- ¼ cup chopped green onion
- 2 cups broccoli flowerets
- 1 cup grated sharp Cheddar cheese
- ¼ cup chopped green pepper
- ¼ cup chopped red pepper

Preheat oven to 450 degrees. For crust, sift flour and salt into a small mixing bowl. Using a pastry blender or 2 knives, cut butter into flour until mixture resembles coarse meal. Sprinkle ice water over dough and mix quickly just until dough forms a soft ball. On a lightly floured surface, use a floured rolling pin to roll out dough into a 12 to 13-inch circle. Press dough into an 11-inch tart pan with removable bottom. Prick bottom of crust with a fork. Trim edges of dough. Bake 10 to 12 minutes or until golden brown. Cool completely before removing crust from pan.

For filling, beat cream cheese in a large bowl until smooth. Add dressing mix, mayonnaise, and sour cream, beating until smooth. Stir in next 3 ingredients. Spread cream cheese mixture into shell. Refrigerate 8 hours or overnight.

Place broccoli flowerets along edge of crust. Sprinkle cheese and peppers over filling, leaving center ungarnished. Slice into wedges and serve chilled.
Yield: 10 to 12 servings

CAJUN CANAPÉS

- 2 cans (10 biscuits per can) refrigerated buttermilk biscuits
- ½ pound mild pork sausage, cooked and drained
- 1½ cups (6 ounces) grated sharp Cheddar cheese
- ¼ cup chopped green pepper
- 2 green onions, chopped
- ¼ cup mayonnaise

Cajun Canapés *(left)* are stuffed with zesty sausage and cheese. Showy yet simple to make, Cornucopia Appetizers have olives and cocktail onions tucked inside rolls of spicy salami and Havarti cheese.

- 2 teaspoons lemon juice
- ½ teaspoon salt
- ½ teaspoon paprika
- ¼ teaspoon cayenne pepper
- ¼ teaspoon garlic powder
- ¼ teaspoon ground thyme

Place biscuits 1 inch apart on greased baking sheet. Following baking time and temperature listed in package directions, bake biscuits, turning halfway through baking time. Allow to cool. Using a melon ball cutter, scoop out center of each biscuit.

Preheat oven to 400 degrees. In a large bowl, mix together remaining ingredients. Spoon about 1 tablespoon of mixture into each hollowed biscuit. Place on baking sheet and bake 8 to 10 minutes or until golden brown and cheese melts. Serve warm.
Yield: 20 canapés

Note: Filled biscuits may be refrigerated overnight before baking. If refrigerated, decrease oven temperature to 325 degrees and bake 12 to 15 minutes or until golden brown and cheese melts.

CORNUCOPIA APPETIZERS

- ½ pound Havarti cheese, sliced paper-thin
- ¼ pound Genoa salami, sliced paper-thin
- 24 cocktail onions
- 24 pimiento-stuffed green olives

Cut cheese slices slightly smaller than salami slices. Place 1 cheese slice on top of each salami slice. Roll into a cone shape. Place 1 onion and 1 olive inside and secure with a toothpick. Refrigerate 1 hour or until firm. Remove toothpick before serving.
Yield: 24 appetizers

CHEESE BLOSSOMS

- 2 cups (8 ounces) grated sharp Cheddar cheese
- 1 cup all-purpose flour
- ½ cup butter or margarine, softened
- 2 tablespoons sesame seeds, toasted
- ½ teaspoon salt
- 1 package (3 ounces) cream cheese, softened
- 3 ounces (½ of 6-ounce package) Kraft® pasteurized process cheese food with garlic

Sliced pimiento-stuffed green olives for garnish

Preheat oven to 375 degrees. Combine first 5 ingredients in a large bowl. Knead with hands, shaping dough into a smooth ball. Cover and refrigerate 1 hour. Shape dough into ¾-inch balls and place on greased baking sheets. Bake 12 to 15 minutes or until light brown. Cool on wire rack.

In a small bowl, blend cream cheese and garlic cheese until smooth; refrigerate 1 hour. Spoon cheese mixture into a decorating bag fitted with a small star tip. Pipe cheese onto biscuits just before serving. Garnish each cheese blossom with 1 slice of olive.

Yield: about 3 dozen cheese blossoms

Rich, buttery Cheese Blossoms look especially festive when garnished with pimiento-stuffed olives.

Stuffed with slices of roast beef and a spicy sauce, Snow Peas with Curry Filling make elegant hors d'oeuvres.

SNOW PEAS WITH CURRY FILLING

- 2 dozen fresh snow pea pods
- ⅛ pound deli roast beef, sliced paper-thin
- 4 ounces (½ of 8-ounce package) cream cheese, softened
- ¼ cup sour cream
- 1 teaspoon curry powder
- ½ teaspoon garlic powder
- ¼ teaspoon granulated sugar

Trim stem and remove strings from sides of each pod. Blanch pea pods in lightly salted boiling water 2 to 3 minutes. Drain and rinse in cold water. Using a sharp knife, slit each pea pod open along straight edge. Cut twenty-four 2 x 3-inch pieces from roast beef. In a small bowl, combine remaining ingredients. Spread about 1 teaspoon of filling in each pea pod; tightly roll a piece of roast beef and insert into pod. Refrigerate 1 hour or until firm.

Yield: about 2 dozen snow peas

POLYNESIAN MEATBALLS

MEATBALLS
1½ pounds ground pork
1¼ pounds ground round
2 cups crushed corn flake cereal
2 eggs, beaten
1 cup milk
3 tablespoons prepared horseradish
3 tablespoons Worcestershire sauce
2 teaspoons dry mustard
1 teaspoon salt
½ teaspoon ground black pepper

SAUCE
1 cup ketchup
½ cup firmly packed brown sugar
½ cup water
⅓ cup soy sauce
2 tablespoons honey
2 tablespoons apple cider vinegar
1 teaspoon dry mustard
1 can (8 ounces) crushed
   pineapple, drained

Preheat oven to 450 degrees. For meatballs, combine all ingredients in a large bowl, mixing well. Shape mixture into 1-inch balls. Place on a rack in a shallow baking pan. Bake 12 to 15 minutes or until brown.

For sauce, mix together all ingredients except pineapple in a large saucepan over medium-high heat. Bring to a boil; reduce heat to medium and simmer 10 minutes. Stir in pineapple. Spoon meatballs into sauce, stirring until well coated. Continue to cook 10 to 15 minutes or until heated through. Serve hot.

Yield: about 75 meatballs

PESTO VEGETABLE DIP

1½ cups chopped fresh parsley
¾ cup grated Parmesan cheese
¼ cup pine nuts
¼ cup olive oil
1 clove garlic
1 cup mayonnaise
1 cup sour cream
1 teaspoon seasoned salt
¼ teaspoon ground black pepper

Fresh vegetables to serve

Place first 4 ingredients in a blender or food processor fitted with a steel blade. Process until mixture resembles coarse meal. Add remaining ingredients and process until smooth. Serve with fresh vegetables.

Yield: about 3 cups of dip

Flavorful Pesto Vegetable Dip is a variation of an Italian favorite. Crushed pineapple lends tropical appeal to Polynesian Meatballs.

Savory Mixed Grill includes morsels of marinated beef, chicken, and shrimp. Served with tangy Cherry Sauce, it satisfies the heartiest of appetites.

MIXED GRILL WITH CHERRY SAUCE

GRILLED MEAT

1¼ pounds boneless, skinless chicken breasts
1½ pounds filet mignon or ribeye steak
1 pound fresh large shrimp
1 cup vegetable oil
1 cup sherry
½ cup soy sauce
3 tablespoons honey
3 cloves garlic, minced
1 teaspoon ground ginger
¼ teaspoon ground black pepper
Wooden skewers

CHERRY SAUCE

⅔ cup plum jam
1 teaspoon soy sauce
¼ teaspoon dry mustard
¼ teaspoon ground ginger
1 can (16 ounces) pitted dark sweet cherries, drained
1 tablespoon cornstarch
2 tablespoons warm water

Cut chicken and beef into ½-inch cubes. Peel and devein shrimp. Place chicken, beef, and shrimp in separate resealable plastic bags. Combine next 7 ingredients in a jar. Secure lid on jar and shake well to mix. Pour ⅓ of marinade into each bag and seal. Refrigerate overnight, turning occasionally. To prevent skewers from burning during cooking, place skewers in a flat dish, cover with water, and soak overnight.

Preheat oven to 375 degrees. Place chicken, beef, and shrimp on soaked skewers. Place on a rack in a roasting pan, loosely cover with aluminum foil, and bake 25 to 30 minutes.

For sauce, place first 4 ingredients in a blender or food processor fitted with steel blade; process until smooth. Add cherries and process briefly to chop. Refrigerate at least 2 hours to allow flavors to blend. Before serving, pour sauce into a small saucepan over medium heat. Combine cornstarch and water in a small bowl and slowly stir into sauce. Cook 3 to 4 minutes or until sauce thickens, stirring frequently. Serve warm with meat.
Yield: about 25 skewers

MERRY CHERRY COCKTAILS

⅔ cup half and half
½ cup cream of coconut
⅓ cup dark rum
⅓ cup cherry brandy
3 tablespoons maraschino cherry
   juice
3 teaspoons grenadine
1½ to 2 cups ice cubes

   Whipped cream and maraschino
   cherries to garnish

Place first 6 ingredients in a blender and mix well. Add ice and blend until frothy. Pour into glasses; garnish with whipped cream and cherries.
Yield: 5 to 6 servings

The surprisingly mild flavor of Nutty Garlic Cheese Spread is enhanced with toasted almonds.

NUTTY GARLIC CHEESE SPREAD

3 heads (about 30 cloves) garlic,
   peeled
2 tablespoons vegetable oil
2 teaspoons white wine vinegar
1½ teaspoons Worcestershire sauce
1 package (8 ounces) cream
   cheese, softened
1¼ cups slivered almonds, toasted
   and finely chopped
1 cup sour cream
¼ cup chopped fresh parsley
½ teaspoon dry mustard
½ teaspoon dried oregano leaves
½ teaspoon salt
¼ teaspoon ground white pepper

   Crackers or bread to serve

Preheat oven to 300 degrees. Place garlic and oil in a shallow baking dish, stirring until well coated. Bake 30 minutes or until light brown. Drain garlic on paper towels and cool completely.
In a blender or food processor fitted with a steel blade, process garlic, vinegar, and Worcestershire sauce until garlic is finely chopped. In a medium bowl, beat cream cheese until smooth. Stir in garlic mixture and remaining ingredients until thoroughly blended. Cover and refrigerate 8 hours or overnight. To serve, bring to room temperature and serve with crackers or bread.
Yield: about 3 cups of spread

A frothy combination of cherry and coconut flavors, Merry Cherry Cocktails are laced with rum and brandy. Dollops of whipped cream and maraschino cherries make festive garnishes.

Hot Cranberry Punch is a delicious blend of cranberry and orange juices, lemonade, and spices. Smoked Oyster Spread *(center)* has a rich, creamy flavor, and Spicy Pastrami Rolls are easy to create with refrigerated crescent rolls.

SPICY PASTRAMI ROLLS

    2 packages (8 ounces each) refrigerated crescent rolls
   ½ pound deli pastrami, sliced paper-thin
   ½ cup soft cream cheese with chives and onions
   ⅓ cup Dijon-style mustard

Preheat oven to 375 degrees. Separate crescent rolls into triangles. Cut triangles in half lengthwise to make 2 smaller triangles. Cut pastrami into 1 x 2-inch strips. Spread 1 teaspoon cream cheese and ½ teaspoon mustard on each triangle, leaving about ¼-inch of the pointed end uncovered. Stack 3 pieces of pastrami at wide end of the triangle. Beginning at the wide end, roll up triangle and place on an ungreased baking sheet with point side down. Bake 12 to 15 minutes or until golden brown. Serve warm.
Yield: 32 rolls

SMOKED OYSTER SPREAD

    2 packages (8 ounces each) cream cheese, softened
   ¼ cup chopped green onion
    2 tablespoons mayonnaise
    1 tablespoon lemon juice
    2 teaspoons prepared horseradish
    2 teaspoons Worcestershire sauce
   ½ teaspoon salt
   ¼ teaspoon onion powder
   ¼ teaspoon hot pepper sauce
    2 cans (3.6 ounces each) smoked oysters, drained and chopped

      Crackers to serve

In a large mixing bowl, beat cream cheese until smooth. Add next 8 ingredients, mixing well. Stir in oysters. Cover and chill 8 hours or overnight. Serve with crackers.
Yield: about 3 cups of spread

HOT CRANBERRY PUNCH

    6 cups cranberry juice
    4 cups orange juice
    1 cup water
    1 can (6 ounces) frozen lemonade concentrate, thawed
   ½ cup firmly packed brown sugar
    3 teaspoons whole cloves
    3 teaspoons ground allspice
    1 whole nutmeg, crushed
    4 3-inch cinnamon sticks, broken into pieces

In a large saucepan or Dutch oven, combine first 5 ingredients. Place spices in a piece of cheesecloth and tie with string; add to punch. Bring to a boil, stirring occasionally. Reduce to low heat, cover, and simmer 30 minutes. Serve hot.
Yield: about 3 quarts of punch

FLORENTINE DIP

1 package (10 ounces) frozen chopped spinach, thawed, drained, and squeezed dry
1 package (3 ounces) cream cheese, softened
½ cup sour cream
2 tablespoons minced green onion
2 teaspoons prepared horseradish
1 jalapeño pepper, seeded and chopped
½ teaspoon salt
¼ teaspoon ground black pepper
½ cup grated sharp Cheddar cheese, divided
½ cup grated Monterey Jack cheese, divided
1 jar (6 ounces) marinated artichoke hearts, drained and chopped

Tortilla Wedges to serve (recipe follows)

Preheat oven to 350 degrees. In a large mixing bowl, combine first 8 ingredients, blending until smooth. Stir in ¼ cup Cheddar and ¼ cup Jack cheese. Spread mixture into a greased 9-inch pie plate. Arrange chopped artichoke hearts around edge of plate. Bake 15 to 20 minutes. Sprinkle remaining cheeses on top and bake 5 minutes longer or until bubbly. Serve warm with Tortilla Wedges.
Yield: about 3 cups of dip

TORTILLA WEDGES

12 large flour tortillas
Vegetable oil

Cut each tortilla into eight wedges. Pour oil into a 10-inch skillet to a depth of ½-inch and heat to 350 degrees. Fry tortilla wedges, 2 at a time, about 10 seconds on each side or until light brown. Drain on paper towels.
Yield: 96 tortilla wedges
Note: Tortilla wedges may be made 1 day in advance and stored in an airtight container.

Light, crispy Tortilla Wedges are the perfect accompaniment for Florentine Dip, a tasteful blend of spinach, cheese, and artichoke hearts.

Holiday Morning Brunch

After the hurry and excitement of opening gifts, a leisurely brunch is a delicious way to relax and enjoy Christmas morning. Whether it's served as a special treat for the family or for company, our menu offers a variety of old favorites along with new dishes to delight everyone. This substantial meal could be your feast for the day — or if you've planned a big dinner for later, you can serve just a few selections for a light breakfast.

A robust combination of meat, spinach, eggs, and cheese is hidden beneath a flaky crust in Hearty Brunch Pie. Holly leaves and colorful berries made from dough make a festive garnish.

HEARTY BRUNCH PIE

CRUST
- 2½ cups all-purpose flour
- ½ teaspoon salt
- ¾ cup plus 2 tablespoons butter, chilled and cut into pieces
- ⅓ cup ice water
- Red food coloring

FILLING
- 1 pound ground turkey
- ½ pound mild pork sausage
- 6 eggs, divided
- 2 packages (10 ounces each) frozen chopped spinach, thawed and squeezed dry
- 4 cups (16 ounces) grated mozzarella cheese
- 1 cup ricotta cheese
- 1 teaspoon salt
- ¼ teaspoon ground black pepper
- 1 tablespoon water

Preheat oven to 375 degrees. For crust, sift flour and salt together into a medium bowl. Using a pastry blender or 2 knives, cut butter into flour until mixture resembles coarse meal. Sprinkle ice water over dough, mixing quickly just until dough forms a soft ball. On a lightly floured surface, use a floured rolling pin to roll out ⅔ of dough into a 16-inch diameter circle. Press dough into a greased 9-inch springform pan. Do not trim edges of dough. Reserve remaining dough for top crust.

For filling, brown turkey and sausage in a large skillet. Drain well and transfer to a large mixing bowl. Reserving 1 yolk, stir in eggs and next 5 ingredients. Spoon filling into springform pan. Fold edge of crust over filling. For top crust, roll out remaining dough to ¼-inch thickness. Cut out a 9-inch diameter circle. Mix reserved egg yolk with water in a small bowl; brush on edge of bottom crust. Place top crust over filling and brush yolk mixture over entire top. For garnish, cut holly leaves from dough scraps and arrange on top of pie. Add 1 teaspoon red food coloring to about 2 tablespoons dough scraps. Form small balls and place in center of holly leaves. Brush garnish with yolk mixture. Bake 1 hour 15 minutes. Cool 10 minutes in pan; remove sides of pan.
Yield: 10 to 12 servings

Dusted with confectioners sugar, Raisin-Eggnog French Toast is a traditional treat with new holiday style.

RAISIN-EGGNOG FRENCH TOAST

- 12 slices raisin bread, dry and firm
- 2 cups prepared eggnog
- ½ cup butter or margarine

  Confectioners sugar to serve

Cut bread into 1-inch wide strips, trimming crusts from any long edges of strips. Pour eggnog into a shallow bowl and dip each strip of bread into the eggnog. Turn each strip over to coat well. Melt butter in a skillet over medium heat. Cook strips of bread on both sides until golden brown. Sprinkle with confectioners sugar before serving.
Yield: about 12 servings

CHOCOLATE-SOUR CREAM COFFEE CAKE

CAKE
    1   cup butter or margarine, softened
    2   cups granulated sugar
    2   eggs
1½   cups cake flour
1½   teaspoons baking powder
    ½   teaspoon salt
    1   cup sour cream
    ½   teaspoon vanilla extract

TOPPING
    1   cup chopped pecans
    2   tablespoons granulated sugar
    1   teaspoon ground cinnamon

CHOCOLATE GLAZE
    ¼   cup butter or margarine
    ½   cup semisweet chocolate chips

Preheat oven to 350 degrees. For cake, cream butter and sugar in a large bowl until fluffy. Add eggs, beating until smooth. In a medium bowl, sift together flour, baking powder, and salt. Gradually add dry ingredients to creamed mixture, blending well. Gently fold in sour cream and vanilla.

For topping, combine all ingredients in a small bowl. For glaze, melt butter and chocolate chips in a small saucepan over low heat, stirring until smooth. Sprinkle 2 tablespoons topping in bottom of greased and floured 9-inch tube pan. Spoon ½ of cake batter into pan. Sprinkle 4 tablespoons topping over batter and drizzle ½ cup glaze over topping. Spoon remaining batter into pan and sprinkle with remaining topping. Reserve remaining glaze. Bake 1 hour to 1 hour 15 minutes or until a toothpick inserted in center comes out clean. Cool 10 minutes in pan. Turn onto serving plate. Drizzle remaining glaze over top of warm cake.

Yield: about 20 servings

Layered with a yummy streusel and chocolate filling, this Chocolate-Sour Cream Coffee Cake is indescribably delicious.

Sunrise Mimosas *(left)* are an eye-opening blend of orange and cranberry juices spiked with vodka, and Candied Pineapple Cookies are loaded with fruit and nuts. Light and elegant, Chilled Asparagus Mousse is enhanced with a hint of dill.

CANDIED PINEAPPLE COOKIES

½ cup butter or margarine, softened
⅓ cup firmly packed brown sugar
2 tablespoons molasses
¼ cup apple juice
2 cups all-purpose flour
2 teaspoons ground cinnamon
½ teaspoon baking soda
1 package (4 ounces) candied pineapple, finely chopped
½ cup chopped walnuts

Preheat oven to 350 degrees. In a large bowl, cream butter and sugar until fluffy. Add molasses and apple juice, beating until smooth. In a medium bowl, sift together flour, cinnamon, and baking soda. Stir dry ingredients into creamed mixture. Stir in candied pineapple and walnuts. Form dough into a ball, cover, and refrigerate 1 hour.

On a lightly floured surface, use a floured rolling pin to roll out dough to ¾-inch thickness. Use a floured 1-inch biscuit cutter to cut out dough. Transfer cookies to a greased baking sheet. Bake 12 to 15 minutes or until light brown.
Yield: about 4 dozen cookies

CHILLED ASPARAGUS MOUSSE

¼ cup butter or margarine
¼ cup all-purpose flour
1½ cups milk, warmed
½ cup whipping cream, warmed
1 envelope unflavored gelatin
¼ cup water
1 teaspoon salt
½ teaspoon ground black pepper
1 tablespoon Dijon-style mustard
1 teaspoon lemon juice
1 teaspoon dill weed
2 packages (8 ounces each) frozen asparagus spears, thawed and drained well

1 large tomato for garnish

Melt butter in a medium saucepan over medium heat; stir in flour. Cook about 2 minutes or until light brown. Add milk and cream, stirring constantly until sauce is thick and smooth. Remove from heat. In a small saucepan, combine gelatin and water over low heat, stirring until gelatin is dissolved. Stir gelatin and next 5 ingredients into sauce. Using a food processor fitted with a steel blade, process asparagus until finely chopped. Stir asparagus into sauce. Pour mixture into a greased 2-quart mold. Chill overnight. To remove from mold, dip in hot water up to rim of mold and invert onto a serving plate.

For rose garnish, remove peel from tomato in 1-inch wide strips. Roll 1 piece of peel into a cone shape, then surround with another piece. Continue with remaining pieces of peel until rose is desired size. Secure with a toothpick and place on top of mousse.
Yield: 12 to 14 servings

SUNRISE MIMOSAS

¾ cup vodka
2½ cups cranberry juice
1½ cups orange juice

Orange slices to garnish

Pour first 3 ingredients into a blender and mix. Pour over ice cubes. Garnish with orange slice on rim of glass.
Yield: 5 to 6 servings

These delicious Pecan Biscuits *(top)* are easy to prepare with packaged baking mix. Chock-full of cheese and bacon, savory Quiche Muffins make nifty little breakfast tidbits.

PECAN BISCUITS

2½ cups biscuit baking mix
½ cup chopped pecans
1 cup whipping cream
2 tablespoons butter or margarine, melted

Preheat oven to 450 degrees. In a large bowl, combine baking mix and pecans. Add cream and stir just until a soft dough forms. On a lightly floured surface, use a floured rolling pin to roll out dough to ½-inch thickness. Use a floured 2-inch biscuit cutter to cut out dough. Transfer biscuits to a greased baking sheet and brush tops with melted butter. Bake 7 to 10 minutes or until light brown.
Yield: about 2 dozen biscuits

QUICHE MUFFINS

1 carton (16 ounces) cottage cheese
3 egg whites
5 eggs
¼ cup buttermilk
¼ cup all-purpose flour
1 teaspoon baking powder
¼ teaspoon salt
2 cups (8 ounces) grated sharp Cheddar cheese
2 green onions, chopped
10 slices bacon, cooked and crumbled

Preheat oven to 400 degrees. Place cottage cheese in a food processor fitted with a steel blade and process until smooth. Transfer to a large bowl Process egg whites in food processor until foamy. Add next 5 ingredients and process until smooth. Add egg mixture to cottage cheese. Stir in cheese, onions, and bacon. Fill greased large muffin tins ⅔ full and bake 12 to 15 minutes or until edges are light brown.
Yield: about 10 muffins

CHEESY GARDEN CASSEROLE

CASSEROLE

- 1 cup diced potato (about 1 medium potato)
- 1 cup diced zucchini squash (about 1 medium squash)
- 1 cup diced carrots (about 3 medium carrots)
- ½ cup diced onion (about 1 medium onion)
- 1 cup water
- ¼ cup all-purpose flour
- ¼ cup butter or margarine
- ¼ teaspoon celery seed
- 1 teaspoon salt
- ¼ teaspoon ground black pepper
- 2 cups milk
- 4 eggs, hard cooked and thinly sliced
- ½ cup grated sharp Cheddar cheese

TOPPING

- ¼ cup butter or margarine
- ¼ cup plain bread crumbs

Preheat oven to 400 degrees. In a large skillet, cook potatoes, squash, carrots, and onions in water over medium-high heat until soft; drain. Reduce heat to medium and return vegetables to skillet. Sprinkle flour over vegetables; stir to blend. Add next 5 ingredients. Cook 10 to 15 minutes, stirring occasionally, until thick. Pour half of vegetable mixture into a greased 9-inch glass pie plate. Top with sliced eggs and pour remaining vegetable mixture over. Sprinkle cheese over vegetable mixture. For topping, melt butter in a small saucepan and stir in bread crumbs. Spread bread crumbs evenly over cheese. Bake 15 to 20 minutes or until cheese is bubbly.

Yield: 8 to 10 servings

Note: Casserole may be assembled 1 day in advance. Cover unbaked casserole and refrigerate. If refrigerated, bake uncovered 25 to 30 minutes or until cheese is bubbly.

SHERRIED FRUIT COBBLER

COBBLER

- 1 can (15½ ounces) sliced pineapple, drained
- 1 can (16 ounces) peach halves, drained
- 1 can (16 ounces) pear halves, drained
- 1 can (16 ounces) apricot halves, drained
- 1 jar (6 ounces) maraschino cherries, drained
- 1 can (21 ounces) apple pie filling
- ½ cup butter
- 2 tablespoons all-purpose flour
- 1 teaspoon ground cinnamon
- ½ teaspoon ground nutmeg
- ¼ teaspoon ground allspice
- ½ cup firmly packed brown sugar
- 1 cup cooking sherry

TOPPING

- ¼ cup butter
- 1 cup graham cracker crumbs

For cobbler, arrange drained fruit and pie filling in a 3-quart casserole dish. Melt butter in a medium saucepan over low heat. Stir in the next 5 ingredients. Slowly add sherry, stirring constantly; cook over medium heat until thickened. Pour over fruit. Cover and chill 8 hours or overnight.

Allow cobbler to come to room temperature. Preheat oven to 350 degrees and bake 20 to 25 minutes or until bubbly. For topping, melt butter in a small saucepan and stir in graham cracker crumbs. Spread crumbs evenly over cobbler and bake 5 minutes longer until crumbs are dark brown.

Yield: about 10 servings

Sherried Fruit Cobbler *(left)* is a mouth-watering mixture of apples, pineapple, peaches, pears, and apricots with brown sugar and sherry. The Cheesy Garden Casserole features a creamy medley of vegetables, eggs, and cheese beneath a layer of toasted bread crumbs.

CAROLING PARTY

From beloved carols to merry choruses, the music of Christmas brings joy to the holidays. An evening of caroling through the neighborhood or singing around the piano draws friends and family together to share the melodies of the season. On such a night, special refreshments are sure to be enjoyed by everyone. Laden with tempting treats and spirited beverages, our festive dessert buffet is a perfect accompaniment for a holiday caroling party.

A wreath of candied cherries makes a festive statement atop this moist Cherry Spice Cake.

CHERRY SPICE CAKE

CAKE

- ½ cup butter or margarine, softened
- 2 cups granulated sugar
- 2 eggs
- 2½ cups all-purpose flour
- 1½ teaspoons baking soda
- 1½ teaspoons ground nutmeg
- 1 teaspoon ground cinnamon
- ½ teaspoon ground cloves
- ½ teaspoon ground allspice
- 1½ cups cherry pie filling

FROSTING

- 16 ounces (two 8-ounce packages) cream cheese, softened
- 1 cup butter or margarine, softened
- 3 tablespoons milk
- 1 tablespoon vanilla extract
- 8 cups sifted confectioners sugar

  Red and green candied cherries to decorate

Preheat oven to 350 degrees. For cake, cream butter and sugar in a large bowl until fluffy. Add eggs, 1 at a time, beating well after each addition. In another large bowl, sift together next 6 ingredients. In a blender or a food processor fitted with a steel blade, process pie filling until cherries are coarsely chopped. Add dry ingredients and pie filling alternately to creamed mixture, mixing until smooth. Pour batter into 3 greased and floured 9-inch round cake pans. Bake 30 to 35 minutes or until a toothpick inserted in center of cake comes out clean. Cool in pans 10 minutes. Turn onto a wire rack to cool completely.

For frosting, combine first 4 ingredients in a large bowl. Add sugar and beat until smooth. Frost between layers, on sides, and on top of cake. Cut candied cherries in half and decorate top of cake with wreath design. Store in refrigerator. Serve at room temperature.

Yield: about 20 servings

Surrounded by a puff pastry crust, Coconut Torte has a delectable coconut-almond filling topped with peach preserves and whipped cream.

COCONUT TORTE

- 1 sheet frozen puff pastry dough, thawed
- 4 eggs
- 1½ cups granulated sugar
- 4½ cups frozen shredded unsweetened coconut, thawed
- 1 cup finely chopped almonds
- 1 tablespoon butter, melted
- 1½ teaspoons vanilla extract
- 1 cup peach preserves
- ½ cup whipping cream

Preheat oven to 350 degrees. On a lightly floured surface, use a floured rolling pin to roll out pastry to a 12-inch diameter circle. Place pastry in a greased 8-inch springform pan. Trim edges of pastry.

In a large bowl, beat eggs until foamy. Gradually add sugar, beating until fluffy. Stir in next 4 ingredients.

Spoon batter into pastry-lined pan. Bake 55 to 60 minutes or until golden brown. Cool in pan 15 minutes. Remove sides of pan and cool completely. Spread peach preserves evenly over top of torte. Whip cream in a small chilled bowl until stiff. Pipe along top edge of torte. Refrigerate until ready to serve.

Yield: about 16 servings

MOCHA MINI PIES

CRUST

- 20 chocolate wafer cookies (2¾-inch diameter)
- 3 tablespoons butter or margarine, cut into pieces

FILLING

- 1 cup milk
- ¾ cup granulated sugar
- 3 tablespoons instant coffee granules
- ¾ cup marshmallow creme
- 2 egg yolks
- 2 cups whipping cream

Preheat oven to 375 degrees. For crust, process chocolate wafers in a blender or food processor fitted with a steel blade until finely crumbled. Add butter and process until mixture resembles coarse meal. Press crumbs into the bottoms of 18 paper-lined muffin tins. Bake 8 to 10 minutes. Cool completely.

For filling, combine milk, sugar, and coffee in a medium saucepan. Cook over medium heat, stirring constantly, until sugar and coffee are dissolved. Add marshmallow creme, stirring until melted. In a small bowl, beat egg yolks until foamy. Add 3 tablespoons marshmallow mixture to yolks and stir. Add yolks to marshmallow mixture and stir until well blended. Pour into a 3-quart bowl and chill until thick but not set (about 45 minutes).

In a medium chilled bowl, whip cream until stiff peaks form; fold into marshmallow mixture, mixing just until filling has a swirled appearance. Pour about ¼ cup filling over each crust. Freeze until firm. Serve frozen.

Yield: 1½ dozen mini pies

PUMPKIN PIE SQUARES

CRUST

- 1¾ cups all-purpose flour
- 1¼ cups granulated sugar
- 2 teaspoons baking powder
- ½ teaspoon salt
- ½ cup plus 2 tablespoons butter or margarine, chilled and cut into pieces
- 2 eggs, beaten

FILLING

- 2 eggs
- ¼ cup firmly packed brown sugar
- 1 can (30 ounces) pumpkin pie mix
- ⅔ cup milk
- 1 tablespoon pumpkin pie spice
- 1 teaspoon ground cinnamon
- 1 teaspoon ground nutmeg

FROSTING

- 1 cup butter or margarine
- 1 cup firmly packed brown sugar
- ½ teaspoon ground cinnamon
- 1½ cups chopped walnuts

Preheat oven to 350 degrees. For crust, sift together first 4 ingredients in a large bowl. Using a pastry blender or 2 knives, cut butter into flour until mixture resembles coarse meal. Add eggs, stirring until a soft dough forms. Press into bottom of a greased 9 x 13-inch baking pan. Bake 15 to 20 minutes or until golden brown.

For filling, beat eggs in a large bowl until foamy. Add sugar, beating until smooth. Stir in remaining ingredients, mixing well. Pour filling over crust. Bake 30 to 40 minutes or until center is set.

For frosting, combine first 3 ingredients in a medium saucepan over medium heat. Stir constantly 3 to 5 minutes or until syrup thickens. Stir in walnuts. Pour frosting evenly over warm filling. Cool completely. Cut into approximately 2-inch squares.

Yield: about 2 dozen squares

Pumpkin Pie Squares (left) are little bites of cake topped with a layer of creamy pumpkin and a luscious praline and walnut frosting. Light and fluffy, frozen Mocha Mini Pies have chocolate cookie crumb crusts.

This smooth Irish Cream Cheesecake is flavored with chocolate and the popular liqueur. A crown of chocolate curls makes a majestic finish.

IRISH CREAM CHEESECAKE

CRUST
- 2 cups finely ground chocolate wafer cookie crumbs (about thirty-six 2¾-inch diameter cookies)
- ¼ cup granulated sugar
- 6 tablespoons butter or margarine, melted

FILLING
- 36 ounces (four and one-half 8-ounce packages) cream cheese, softened
- 1⅔ cups granulated sugar
- 5 eggs
- 1½ cups Irish Cream liqueur
- 1 tablespoon vanilla extract
- 1 cup (6 ounces) semisweet chocolate chips

TOPPING
- 1 cup whipping cream
- 2 tablespoons granulated sugar
- ½ cup (3 ounces) semisweet chocolate chips, melted

CHOCOLATE CURLS
- 2 cups (12 ounces) semisweet chocolate chips

Preheat oven to 325 degrees. For crust, combine crumbs and sugar in a large bowl. Add butter, stirring until mixture resembles coarse meal. Press into bottom and 1 inch up sides of a greased 9-inch springform pan. Bake 7 to 10 minutes.

For filling, beat cream cheese until smooth. Add sugar and eggs, beating until fluffy. Add liqueur and vanilla,

mixing well. Sprinkle chocolate chips over crust. Spoon filling over chocolate chips. Bake 1 hour 20 minutes to 1 hour 30 minutes or until center is set. Cool completely in pan. Remove sides of pan.

For topping, beat cream and sugar in a large chilled bowl until stiff. Continue to beat while slowly adding chocolate. Spread mixture over cooled cake.

For chocolate curls, melt chocolate in a small saucepan over low heat. Pour onto a baking sheet. Let stand at room temperature until set but not firm. To make curls, pull a cheese plane across surface of chocolate (curls will break if chocolate is too firm). Remelt and cool chocolate as necessary to form desired number of curls. Arrange on cake. Refrigerate until ready to serve.

Yield: about 16 servings

Warm and creamy with a hint of coconut, Hot Cappuccino Punch is laced with rum and brandy. It's a perfect complement to flaky Raisin-Walnut Pinwheels.

RAISIN-WALNUT PINWHEELS

1 sheet frozen puff pastry dough, thawed
⅓ cup granulated sugar
1 tablespoon ground cinnamon
¼ cup butter or margarine
½ cup raisins
½ cup finely chopped walnuts
1 egg yolk, beaten

Preheat oven to 350 degrees. On a lightly floured surface, use a floured rolling pin to roll out pastry to an 8 x 12-inch rectangle. In a small bowl, combine sugar and cinnamon and set aside. In a small saucepan, melt butter. Add raisins and walnuts, stirring until well coated. Spread raisin mixture evenly over pastry. Sprinkle sugar mixture evenly over raisin mixture. Beginning at 1 long edge, roll up pastry. Brush egg yolk on long edge to seal. Bake on a greased baking sheet 20 to 25 minutes or until golden brown. Cool completely. Cut into 1-inch thick slices.
Yield: about 12 pinwheels

HOT CAPPUCCINO PUNCH

3 cups brewed coffee, room temperature
3 cups half and half
½ cup cream of coconut
½ cup rum
½ cup brandy

Combine all ingredients in a large saucepan. Cook over medium heat until mixture begins to boil. Remove from heat. Serve immediately.
Yield: 7 to 8 servings

MACADAMIA NUT FUDGE TART

CRUST

1¾ cups all-purpose flour
⅓ cup cocoa
⅛ teaspoon salt
¼ cup granulated sugar
¾ cup butter or margarine, chilled
    and cut into pieces
½ cup strong cold coffee

FILLING

1 package (6 ounces) semisweet
    chocolate chips, melted
⅔ cup granulated sugar
2 tablespoons butter or margarine,
    melted
2 tablespoons milk
2 teaspoons coffee-flavored liqueur
2 eggs, beaten
½ cup chopped macadamia nuts

For crust, combine first 4 ingredients in a large bowl. Using a pastry blender or 2 knives, cut butter into dry ingredients until mixture resembles coarse meal. Add coffee and knead until a soft dough forms. Cover and chill 8 hours or overnight. On a lightly floured surface, use a floured rolling pin to roll out dough to an 11-inch diameter circle. Press into a greased 9-inch tart pan. Chill at least 1 hour.

Preheat oven to 350 degrees. For filling, mix together first 5 ingredients in a large bowl. Add eggs, beating until smooth. Fold in nuts. Pour batter into tart shell. Bake 30 to 40 minutes or until top is dry and firm (inside will be soft). Cool completely in pan.
Yield: about 16 servings

BLACKBERRY CORDIAL

1 cup club soda, chilled
⅔ cup crème de cassis
½ cup raspberry-flavored liqueur
½ cup blackberry-flavored brandy

Frozen blackberries to garnish

Combine all ingredients in a large bowl, mixing well. Serve chilled. Garnish with frozen blackberries.
Yield: about 6 servings

Nestled in a cocoa-mocha crust, Macadamia Nut Fudge Tart is a chocolate lover's delight! Sparkling Blackberry Cordial has a fruity kick.

An incredible date and pecan frosting makes this three-layer Chocolate-Date Nut Cake extra special. Chocolate Mocha Brownies are studded with chunks of white and semisweet chocolate.

CHOCOLATE-DATE NUT CAKE

CAKE

1 cup butter or margarine, softened
2 cups granulated sugar
3 eggs
½ cup cocoa
½ cup hot water
1 cup boiling coffee
1 teaspoon vanilla extract
3 cups all-purpose flour
1 teaspoon baking soda
½ teaspoon salt
1 cup finely chopped pecans

FROSTING

3 cups granulated sugar
1 can (14 ounces) sweetened condensed milk
½ cup hot water
2 cups chopped dates (about 1 pound)
1 cup finely chopped pecans

Preheat oven to 350 degrees. For cake, cream butter and sugar in a large bowl until fluffy. Add eggs and beat until smooth. In a small bowl, dissolve cocoa in hot water. Add cocoa, coffee, and vanilla to creamed mixture and mix well. In a large bowl, sift together next 3 ingredients. Add dry ingredients to creamed mixture, beating until smooth. Fold in pecans. Pour batter into 3 greased and floured 9-inch round cake pans. Bake 25 to 30 minutes or until a toothpick inserted in center of cake comes out clean. Cool in pan 10 minutes. Turn onto a wire rack to cool.

For frosting, combine sugar, milk, and water in a medium saucepan. Bring to a boil over medium-high heat. Reduce heat to medium and cook 5 to 8 minutes, stirring constantly, until frosting thickens. Stir in dates and pecans. Frost between layers, on sides, and on top of cake.

Yield: about 20 servings

CHOCOLATE MOCHA BROWNIES

1 cup firmly packed brown sugar
¾ cup butter or margarine
2 tablespoons instant coffee
1 tablespoon hot water
2 eggs
2 tablespoons vanilla extract
2 cups all-purpose flour
2 teaspoons baking powder
½ teaspoon salt
4 ounces semisweet chocolate, broken into small pieces
4 ounces white chocolate, broken into small pieces

In a medium saucepan, melt sugar and butter over medium-low heat. Dissolve coffee in hot water and stir into butter mixture. Cool to room temperature.

Preheat oven to 350 degrees. Beat eggs and vanilla into butter mixture. In a large bowl, sift together next 3 ingredients. Stir butter mixture into dry ingredients. Fold in chocolate chunks. Pour batter into a greased 8 x 11-inch baking pan. Bake 25 to 30 minutes or until light brown. Cool in pan. Cut into 1½-inch squares.

Yield: about 3 dozen brownies

GINGER POUND CAKE

CAKE

- 1½ cups butter or margarine, softened
- 2¼ cups firmly packed brown sugar
- ½ cup granulated sugar
- 5 eggs
- 2 teaspoons vanilla extract
- 3 cups all-purpose flour
- 1 tablespoon ground ginger
- ½ teaspoon baking powder
- ¼ teaspoon salt
- 1 cup milk
- 1 cup chopped walnuts

GLAZE

- 16 marshmallows
- ⅔ cup apple jelly
- ¼ cup lemon juice
- ¼ cup butter or margarine, cut into pieces

Walnut halves to garnish

Preheat oven to 350 degrees. For cake, cream butter and sugars in a large bowl until fluffy. Add eggs 1 at a time, beating well after each addition. Beat in vanilla. In another large bowl, sift together next 4 ingredients. Add milk and dry ingredients alternately to creamed mixture. Fold in nuts. Pour batter into a greased and floured 10-inch tube pan. Bake 1 hour 10 minutes to 1 hour 20 minutes or until a toothpick inserted in center of cake comes out clean. Cool in pan 15 minutes. Turn onto a wire rack to cool completely.

For glaze, combine marshmallows, jelly, and lemon juice in a medium saucepan over low heat, stirring until glaze is smooth. Add butter 1 piece at a time, whisking until melted. Drizzle glaze over top of cake and garnish with walnut halves.

Yield: about 20 servings

EGGNOG MOUSSE

- 1 teaspoon unflavored gelatin
- 1 tablespoon hot water
- 1 cup prepared eggnog
- 1 tablespoon butter or margarine
- 1 teaspoon vanilla extract
- 1 tablespoon rum
- 1 cup whipping cream

Ground nutmeg to garnish

In a small bowl, soften gelatin in water. In a small saucepan, combine eggnog and butter over low heat. Stirring constantly, cook until butter is melted. Add gelatin and continue to stir

Mild, nutty Ginger Pound Cake is enhanced with a tangy apple-lemon glaze. Creamy Eggnog Mousse is a new way to enjoy a favorite holiday flavor.

until gelatin is dissolved. Remove from heat and stir in vanilla and rum. Cool to room temperature. In a large chilled bowl, beat cream until stiff. Fold eggnog mixture into cream. Pour into individual bowls and chill until set. Garnish with nutmeg.

Yield: about 4 servings of mousse

Santa's Sweetshop

As the holidays draw near, the magic of Christmas fills the air. In a flurry of activity, we prepare the scrumptious cookies and confections that add such cheer to the season. Young and old alike eagerly await the fun of sampling each treat fresh from the kitchen. The sweets in this collection are so delicious that everyone will think they're from Santa's own sweetshop at the North Pole!

Cut in the shape of trees and coated with colorful icing, these buttery Christmas Lemon Cookies have lots of holiday appeal. Silvery dragées make pretty "ornaments" for the trees.

CHRISTMAS LEMON COOKIES

COOKIES
1 cup butter or margarine, softened
½ cup granulated sugar
1 teaspoon grated dried lemon peel
2½ cups all-purpose flour

ICING
2¼ cups confectioners sugar
5 tablespoons milk

Red and green paste food coloring
Dragées

For cookies, cream butter, sugar, and lemon peel in a large bowl until fluffy. Stir in flour; knead dough until a soft ball forms. Cover and chill 30 minutes. Preheat oven to 300 degrees. On a lightly floured surface, use a floured rolling pin to roll out dough to ¼-inch thickness. Use a tree-shaped cookie cutter to cut out dough. Transfer cookies to a greased baking sheet. Bake 20 to 25 minutes or until cookies are light brown. Cool on wire rack.

For icing, mix sugar and milk together in a medium bowl (icing will be thin). Divide icing evenly into 3 small bowls. Tint 1 bowl red and 1 bowl green; leave 1 bowl white. Pour icing over tops of cookies, smoothing with a spatula. Decorate with dragées. Allow icing to harden. Store in an airtight container.
Yield: about 3 dozen 5-inch cookies

BUTTER PECAN COOKIES

½ cup plus 2 tablespoons butter, softened and divided
1½ cups coarsely chopped pecans
½ cup granulated sugar, divided
6 tablespoons firmly packed brown sugar
1 egg
½ teaspoon vanilla extract
1½ cups all-purpose flour
½ teaspoon baking soda
½ teaspoon salt

Preheat oven to 375 degrees. In a large skillet, melt 2 tablespoons butter over medium heat. Stir in pecans and cook 10 to 15 minutes or until nuts are dark brown. Remove from heat and stir in 2 tablespoons granulated sugar. Cool to room temperature.

Cream remaining butter and sugars in a large bowl until fluffy. Beat in egg and vanilla. Sift next 3 ingredients into a small bowl. Add dry ingredients to creamed mixture, stirring until a soft dough forms. Fold in pecans. Drop by tablespoonfuls onto a greased baking sheet. Bake 8 to 10 minutes or until edges are brown. Cool on wire rack. Store in an airtight container.
Yield: about 2 dozen cookies

Sent special delivery from the North Pole, brown-sugary Butter Pecan Cookies are packed with nuts.

Santa would love these treats on Christmas Eve: Checkerboard Walnuts (*left*) are luscious bites of coconut covered with vanilla or chocolate candy coating, and Raspberry Nut Bars have a jam filling.

CHECKERBOARD WALNUTS

 2 cups flaked coconut
 2 tablespoons light corn syrup
 ½ cup granulated sugar
 ⅛ teaspoon salt
 1 egg white
 ¼ teaspoon coconut extract
 24 walnut halves
 4 ounces chocolate-flavored almond bark
 4 ounces vanilla-flavored almond bark

In a large saucepan, combine coconut, corn syrup, sugar, and salt. Cook over medium heat, stirring constantly, 5 to 6 minutes or until candy thickens and coconut is light brown. Whisk egg white in a small bowl until foamy. Add egg white to coconut mixture. Stirring constantly, cook 5 to 6 minutes longer or until mixture becomes stiff and very sticky. Remove from heat and stir in coconut extract. Cool to room temperature. Dip fingers in cold water and shape coconut mixture into 1-inch balls. Place on waxed paper; press 1 walnut half on top of each coconut ball. Refrigerate 1 hour or until firm.

Melt vanilla and chocolate almond bark in separate small saucepans following package directions. Dip bottom half of each candy in chocolate or vanilla bark, completely covering coconut. Return to waxed paper and cool completely. Store at room temperature in an airtight container.
Yield: about 2 dozen candies

RASPBERRY NUT BARS

 1½ cups butter or margarine, softened
 2 cups granulated sugar
 2 egg yolks
 1 teaspoon vanilla extract
 4 cups all-purpose flour
 1⅓ cups finely chopped pecans
 1 jar (12 ounces) raspberry preserves

Preheat oven to 350 degrees. In a large bowl, cream butter and sugar until fluffy. Beat in egg yolks and vanilla. Mix in flour and pecans, stirring until a soft dough forms.

Divide dough in half. Press half of dough into a greased 9 x 13-inch glass baking pan. Spread preserves evenly over dough. Place remaining dough on a sheet of waxed paper. Dust with flour and use a floured rolling pin to roll out dough to 9 x 13-inch rectangle. Place dough over preserves, patching if necessary to completely cover preserves. Bake 40 to 45 minutes or until golden brown. Cool completely in pan. Cut into 1 x 3-inch bars. Store in an airtight container.
Yield: about 3 dozen bars

HAZELNUT LACE COOKIES

- ½ cup butter or margarine, softened
- ½ cup firmly packed brown sugar
- 2 tablespoons dark rum, divided
- 2 tablespoons whipping cream
- ⅓ cup semisweet chocolate chips
- ¼ cup all-purpose flour
- ¼ teaspoon salt
- ⅛ teaspoon baking soda
- 1 cup quick-cooking rolled oats
- ½ cup flaked coconut
- ½ cup finely chopped hazelnuts

Purchased red decorating icing

Preheat oven to 350 degrees. In a large bowl, cream butter and sugar until fluffy. Beat in 1 tablespoon rum. In a small saucepan, heat cream over medium heat until boiling. Reduce heat to medium-low. Stir in remaining rum and simmer 2 to 3 minutes. Remove from heat; add chocolate chips and stir until mixture is smooth. Beat chocolate mixture into creamed mixture until smooth. In a large bowl, sift flour, salt, and baking soda together. Stir dry ingredients into chocolate mixture. Fold in oats, coconut, and hazelnuts. Drop batter by rounded teaspoonfuls 4 inches apart onto a greased baking sheet. Use fingers to press each cookie into a 2-inch diameter circle. Bake 8 minutes (cookies will be soft). Remove from oven and cool on pan 5 minutes. Cool completely on a wire rack. Decorate with icing. Allow icing to harden. Store in an airtight container.
Yield: about 3½ dozen cookies

MACADAMIA NUT TARTS

CRUST
- 1½ cups butter or margarine, softened
- ⅔ cup granulated sugar
- 2½ teaspoons grated dried lemon peel
- 3 cups all-purpose flour
- ½ cup cornstarch
- ½ teaspoon salt

TOPPING
- ½ cup plus 2 tablespoons butter or margarine
- ½ cup firmly packed brown sugar
- ⅓ cup honey
- 3 cups macadamia nuts
- 2½ tablespoons whipping cream

Preheat oven to 350 degrees. For crust, cream butter, sugar, and lemon peel in a large bowl until fluffy. In a medium bowl, sift together next 3 ingredients. Stir dry ingredients into

A hint of rum makes these delicate Hazelnut Lace Cookies *(top)* extra special. Macadamia Nut Tarts feature luscious caramel-coated nuts heaped in a pastry shell.

creamed mixture, mixing just until dough is crumbly. On a lightly floured surface, use a floured rolling pin to roll out dough to ¼-inch thickness. Use a 3-inch biscuit cutter to cut out dough. Transfer dough to greased 2½-inch diameter tart pans. Prick with a fork. Bake 16 to 18 minutes or until light brown. Cool in pan 10 minutes; turn onto a wire rack to cool completely.

For topping, combine first 3 ingredients in a medium saucepan. Stir constantly over medium-high heat until mixture comes to a boil. Boil 1 minute without stirring until mixture thickens and large bubbles begin to form. Remove from heat; stir in nuts and cream. Spoon about 2 tablespoons mixture into each tart crust. Cool completely.
Yield: about 20 tarts

BAKED BANANA SQUARES

CRUST
1¼ cups graham cracker crumbs
¼ cup granulated sugar
¼ cup butter or margarine, melted

TOPPING
¼ cup butter or margarine
1 teaspoon grated dried lemon peel
1 tablespoon lemon juice
4 firm bananas, cut into ½-inch slices
¼ cup firmly packed brown sugar

Preheat oven to 375 degrees. For crust, combine all ingredients in a medium bowl, mixing well. Press into the bottom of a greased 8-inch square pan. Bake 5 to 6 minutes or until brown.

For topping, melt butter in a medium saucepan over low heat. Add next 3 ingredients and stir until bananas are coated with butter. Arrange banana slices on crust. Sprinkle brown sugar over bananas and bake 12 to 15 minutes or until bubbly. Cut into 2-inch squares. Serve warm.
Yield: about 16 squares

Nestled on a graham cracker crust, Baked Banana Squares are sprinkled with brown sugar and served warm for a yummy treat.

PUMPKIN-WALNUT COOKIES

COOKIES
1 cup butter or margarine, softened
1 cup granulated sugar
1 cup canned pumpkin
1 egg
1 teaspoon vanilla extract
2 cups all-purpose flour
1 teaspoon baking powder
1 teaspoon ground cinnamon
½ teaspoon ground nutmeg
½ teaspoon baking soda
½ teaspoon salt
¼ teaspoon ground allspice
1 cup raisins
1 cup chopped walnuts

ICING
1 package (3 ounces) cream cheese, softened

1 cup confectioners sugar
2 tablespoons water

Preheat oven to 350 degrees. For cookies, cream butter and sugar in a large bowl until fluffy. Add next 3 ingredients, mixing well. In a medium bowl, sift together next 7 ingredients. Add to creamed mixture, mixing well. Stir in raisins and nuts. Drop by rounded teaspoonfuls onto greased baking sheet. Bake 12 to 15 minutes or until light brown. Cool on a wire rack. For icing, mix all ingredients in a small bowl until smooth. Drizzle icing over cooled cookies. Allow icing to harden. Store in an airtight container.
Yield: about 7 dozen cookies

Pumpkin-Walnut Cookies have a moist, cake-like texture similar to pumpkin bread.

Kids of all ages will love these goodies: Lightly sweetened Christmas Honey Grahams are cut in holiday shapes, and Peanut Butter Crunch Balls are studded with colorful candies. Cashew Toffee is topped with semisweet chocolate.

CHRISTMAS HONEY GRAHAMS

- 1½ cups whole wheat graham flour
- 1 cup all-purpose flour
- ½ cup vegetable shortening
- ⅓ cup firmly packed brown sugar
- ¼ cup honey
- ¼ cup vegetable oil
- 3 tablespoons cold water
- 1 teaspoon baking soda
- 1 teaspoon ground cinnamon
- ½ teaspoon salt

Combine all ingredients in a large bowl; knead dough until a soft ball forms. Cover and refrigerate 30 minutes. Preheat oven to 425 degrees. On a lightly floured surface, use a floured rolling pin to roll out dough to ¼-inch thickness. Use desired cookie cutters to cut out dough. Transfer crackers to an ungreased baking sheet and prick with a fork. Bake 7 to 10 minutes or until golden brown. Cool on baking sheet (crackers will become crisp as they cool). Store in an airtight container.
Yield: about 1½ dozen 5-inch crackers

CASHEW TOFFEE

- 40 saltine crackers with unsalted tops
- 1 cup butter or margarine
- 1 cup firmly packed brown sugar
- 2 cups chopped unsalted cashews
- 1 package (12 ounces) semisweet chocolate chips

Preheat oven to 400 degrees. Arrange a single layer of crackers with sides touching in the bottom of a foil-lined 11 x 17-inch shallow baking pan. In a small saucepan, combine butter and sugar over medium heat. Cook, stirring constantly, until syrup reaches hard ball stage (250 to 268 degrees). Remove from heat and stir in cashews. Pour syrup over crackers and bake 5 minutes. Remove from oven and sprinkle chocolate chips evenly over crackers. As chocolate melts, spread evenly over candy. Refrigerate 30 minutes or until candy hardens. Break candy into pieces. Store at room temperature in an airtight container.
Yield: about 1 pound of candy

PEANUT BUTTER CRUNCH BALLS

- 4 cups miniature marshmallows
- ½ cup butter or margarine
- ½ cup creamy peanut butter
- 3 cups toasted oat cereal
- 1 cup unsalted peanuts
- 1 cup red and green candy-coated chocolate pieces

In a medium saucepan, melt first 3 ingredients over low heat, stirring constantly until smooth. Remove from heat. Cool 15 minutes. In a large bowl, mix remaining ingredients. Pour syrup over cereal mixture, stirring until evenly coated. Roll mixture into 2-inch balls and cool completely on waxed paper. Store in an airtight container.
Yield: about 3 dozen crunch balls

MARMALADE COOKIES

- 2 cups all-purpose flour
- 1 teaspoon baking powder
- 1 cup butter or margarine, chilled and cut into pieces
- 1 cup finely ground almonds
- ¾ cup granulated sugar
- 2 tablespoons lemon juice
- ½ cup orange marmalade
- 6 ounces chocolate-flavored almond bark

Preheat oven to 375 degrees. In a large bowl, sift flour and baking powder together. With a pastry blender or 2 knives, cut butter into flour until mixture resembles coarse meal. Stir in next 3 ingredients; knead dough until a soft ball forms. Cover and chill 1 hour. On a lightly floured surface, use a floured rolling pin to roll out dough to ⅛-inch thickness. Use a 3-inch round cookie cutter to cut out 48 cookies. Transfer cookies to a greased baking sheet and bake 10 to 12 minutes or until light brown. Cool on baking sheet. Spread marmalade on half the cookies; top with remaining cookies. In a small saucepan, melt almond bark following package directions. Dip half of each sandwich cookie into the chocolate. Cool on waxed paper.

Yield: 2 dozen cookies

CHERRY CORDIAL FUDGE

- ¾ cup milk
- 2 cups granulated sugar
- 2 ounces unsweetened chocolate
- 2 tablespoons light corn syrup
- 2 tablespoons butter or margarine, cut into small pieces
- 1 jar (6 ounces) maraschino cherries, drained and halved
- 2 teaspoons vanilla extract

In a medium saucepan, combine first 4 ingredients. Cook over medium heat, stirring constantly, until mixture is smooth and comes to a boil. Reduce heat to low, cover pan, and boil 2 to 3 minutes. Uncover and stir to blend ingredients. Continue to boil uncovered, without stirring, until syrup reaches soft ball stage (234 to 240 degrees). Remove from heat. Drop in butter; do not stir until syrup cools to 110 degrees. Add cherries and vanilla, stirring until mixture thickens and is no longer glossy. Pour into a greased 8-inch square pan. Chill until firm; cut into 1-inch squares.

Yield: 64 squares of fudge

Light up the season with these fruity delights: Spread with orange marmalade and dipped in chocolate, Marmalade Cookies *(in tin)* taste as good as they look. Tiny Apricot Foldovers have a sweet filling of dried fruit, and Cherry Cordial Fudge is a rich blend of chocolate and maraschino cherries.

APRICOT FOLDOVERS

FILLING
- 1 cup chopped dried apricots
- 1 cup firmly packed brown sugar
- ½ cup water
- 2 tablespoons all-purpose flour

PASTRY
- 2½ cups all-purpose flour
- ½ teaspoon salt
- ¾ cup plus 2 tablespoons butter or margarine, chilled and cut into pieces
- 1 package (3 ounces) cream cheese, cut into pieces
- ⅓ cup ice water

For filling, mix all ingredients together in a medium saucepan over medium heat and bring to a boil. Cook, stirring constantly, 8 to 10 minutes or until filling thickens. Cool completely.

Preheat oven to 350 degrees. For pastry, sift flour and salt together into a medium bowl. Using a pastry blender or 2 knives, cut butter and cream cheese into flour until mixture resembles coarse meal. Sprinkle ice water over dough, mixing quickly just until dough forms a soft ball. On a lightly floured surface, use a floured rolling pin to roll out dough into a ¼-inch thick rectangle. Use a pastry wheel to cut dough into 2-inch squares. Transfer dough to a greased baking sheet. Spoon about 1 teaspoon of filling into the center of each square. Fold dough in half diagonally over filling to form a triangle; use a fork to crimp edges together. Bake 15 to 20 minutes or until golden brown. Cool completely on a wire rack. Store in an airtight container.

Yield: about 4 dozen cookies

CHOCOLATE BRANDY DROPS

- 1 cup butter or margarine, softened
- 1 cup confectioners sugar
- ½ cup granulated sugar
- 1 cup semisweet chocolate chips, chilled
- 3 cups all-purpose flour
- 1½ cups brandy
- 1 cup finely chopped pecans

Preheat oven to 350 degrees. In a large bowl, cream butter and sugars until fluffy. In a food processor fitted with a steel blade, process chocolate chips until finely chopped. Add chocolate and remaining ingredients to creamed mixture, stirring until a soft dough forms. Drop by teaspoonfuls onto greased baking sheet. Bake 12 to 15 minutes or until light brown. Cool completely on a wire rack. Store in an airtight container.

Yield: about 3 dozen cookies

SCOTCHIES

- 1 cup butter or margarine, softened
- 1 cup confectioners sugar
- 6 tablespoons Scotch whiskey
- 2½ cups all-purpose flour
- ½ cup butterscotch chips, chilled
- 1 cup finely chopped pecans
  Confectioners sugar

Preheat oven to 350 degrees. In a large bowl, cream butter and sugar until fluffy. Add whiskey and flour, stirring until a soft dough forms. In a food processor fitted with a steel blade, process butterscotch chips until finely chopped. Stir chopped chips and pecans into dough. Shape tablespoonfuls of dough into crescent shapes and place on greased baking sheet. Bake 12 to 15 minutes or until light brown. Roll cookies in confectioners sugar immediately after removing from oven. Cool completely on a wire rack. Roll in confectioners sugar again.

Yield: about 4½ dozen cookies

CHOCOLATE-RAISIN TOFFEE

- 1 cup raisins
- ¾ cup butter
- 1 cup firmly packed brown sugar
- 1 cup semisweet chocolate chips

Spread raisins evenly on a greased 10 x 15-inch shallow baking pan. Melt butter and sugar in a medium saucepan. Cook over medium heat, stirring constantly, until syrup reaches hard crack stage (300 to 310 degrees). Pour syrup over raisins. Top with chocolate chips. As chocolate melts, spread evenly over raisins. Cool and cut into 1½-inch squares. Store at room temperature.

Yield: about 5 dozen pieces of candy

A creamy-crunchy combination, Chocolate-Raisin Toffee *(left)* is sure to be a favorite any time of the year. Chocolate Brandy Drops *(center)* will melt in your mouth, and crispy Scotchies are flavored with butterscotch and Scotch whiskey.

Gifts From The Kitchen

Sharing good things from your kitchen is one of the joys of the Christmas season, and a creative presentation makes each gift extra special. An attractive basket, a painted tin, or simply a pretty bow can transform each gift into a unique offering. This collection of food gifts includes festive recipes and lots of fun ideas for decorating and packaging them. Presented with love, your thoughtful gifts are sure to be appreciated.

Festive cookies make merry gifts! The Country Santa Cookies are maple-flavored triangles decorated with colorful icing. For wholesome snacks or delightful party favors, spicy Christmas Tree Cookies are perched atop rosy red apples and adorned with bows.

CHRISTMAS TREE COOKIES

- ½ cup vegetable shortening
- ½ cup butter or margarine, softened
- 1½ cups firmly packed brown sugar
- 1 egg
- ⅓ cup evaporated milk
- ½ teaspoon vanilla extract
- 3½ cups all-purpose flour
- 1 teaspoon baking powder
- ½ teaspoon ground cinnamon
- ½ teaspoon ground cloves
- ½ teaspoon ground ginger
- ½ teaspoon salt
- 18 6-inch wooden skewers
- 18 apples

In a large bowl, cream shortening, butter, and sugar until fluffy. Add next 3 ingredients, mixing until smooth. In another large bowl, sift together next 6 ingredients. Add dry ingredients to creamed mixture; knead until a soft dough forms. Cover and refrigerate at least 1 hour.

Preheat oven to 350 degrees. On a lightly floured surface, use a floured rolling pin to roll out dough to ¼-inch thickness. Use a tree-shaped cookie cutter to cut out cookies. Transfer cookies to a greased baking sheet. Insert a skewer into bottom of each tree, leaving 2 inches of skewer exposed. Bake 8 to 10 minutes or until golden brown. Cool completely. Insert skewer into top of apple.
Yield: 1½ dozen 5-inch cookies

COUNTRY SANTA COOKIES

COOKIES
- 1 cup butter or margarine, softened
- 3 packages (3 ounces each) cream cheese, softened
- 2 eggs, beaten
- 1 teaspoon maple extract
- 3 cups all-purpose flour
- 2 teaspoons baking powder
- 1 cup granulated sugar
- ¼ teaspoon salt

ICING
- 4 cups confectioners sugar
- 6 tablespoons milk
  Red and green paste food coloring
  Purchased white decorating icing

For cookies, beat butter and cream cheese in a large bowl until smooth. Mix in eggs and maple extract. In another large bowl, sift together next 4

This Chocolate-Mint Dessert Spread will delight chocolate lovers! Shaped into a ball and rolled in chopped pecans, it's delicious served on crispy chocolate cookie wafers. For a gift with country flair, present the spread and some wafers in a basket lined with a reversible cloth.

ingredients. Blend flour mixture into butter mixture. Cover and chill at least 1 hour.

Preheat oven to 375 degrees. On a lightly floured surface, use a floured rolling pin to roll out dough to ¼-inch thickness. Trace pattern onto tracing paper and cut out. Place pattern on dough and use a sharp knife to cut around pattern. Transfer cookies to a greased baking sheet. Bake 10 to 12 minutes or until light brown.

For icing, beat sugar and milk together in a large bowl. Divide icing in half. Tint red and green. Spread icing on cookies for coat and hat. Use decorating icing to decorate cookies.
Yield: about 3 dozen cookies

CHOCOLATE-MINT DESSERT SPREAD

- 1½ cups (9 ounces) semisweet chocolate chips, melted
- ½ cup crème de menthe liqueur
- 3 packages (8 ounces each) cream cheese, softened
- 1 teaspoon ground cinnamon
- 2 cups finely chopped pecans

  Chocolate cookie wafers to serve

In a large bowl, mix together first 4 ingredients until smooth. Cover and chill 1 hour. Divide mixture into thirds and form into balls. Roll balls in pecans. Serve with chocolate cookie wafers. Store in refrigerator.
Yield: 3 dessert balls

Coated with spices and brown sugar, this crunchy Cinnamon Nut Mix is a great gift for all your "deers." The painted Snowflake Tin and whimsical tag will spark the spirit of the season in everyone.

CINNAMON NUT MIX

       2 cups whole almonds
       2 cups pecan halves
       6 cups water
       1 cup granulated sugar
       1 cup firmly packed brown sugar
    ¼ cup ground cinnamon
       1 tablespoon ground ginger
       2 teaspoons ground allspice
       1 teaspoon ground cloves
       2 egg whites

Preheat oven to 300 degrees. In a large saucepan, cover almonds and pecans with water. Bring to a boil, reduce heat to medium-low, and simmer 1 minute. Drain well. In a large bowl, combine next 6 ingredients. In a medium bowl, whisk egg whites until foamy. Add nuts and stir until nuts are well coated. Pour nuts into sugar mixture, stirring until well coated. Spread evenly on a greased baking sheet. Stirring occasionally, bake 25 to 30 minutes. Cool completely on baking sheet. Store in an airtight container.
Yield: about 4 cups of nuts

SNOWFLAKE TIN

You will need desired metal tin, red spray paint, white acrylic paint, spray paint primer, and a small paintbrush.

1. Apply 1 coat of primer to tin; allow to dry.
2. Apply 1 coat of red paint to tin; allow to dry.
3. Referring to photo, use paintbrush and white paint to paint snowflakes on tin; allow to dry.

During the holidays, warm hearts with a gift of Brown Sugar Shortbread or Spiced Coffee Mix. By using the shape of your gift box to create a pattern for cutting out the nutty cookies, you can give them a custom look. The coffee mix, which can be presented in a Christmasy mug, is a delicious addition to hot beverages.

BROWN SUGAR SHORTBREAD

    2 cups all-purpose flour
    1 cup pecans
    ⅛ teaspoon salt
    1 cup butter or margarine, softened
    ½ cup firmly packed brown sugar

Place flour, pecans, and salt in a blender or food processor fitted with a steel blade. Process until mixture is a fine powder. In a large bowl, cream butter and sugar until fluffy. Mix dry ingredients into creamed mixture; knead until a soft dough forms. Cover and chill 8 hours or overnight.

Preheat oven to 300 degrees. For cookie pattern, place desired gift box on tracing paper. Use a pencil to draw around box. Cut out pattern ⅜ inch inside drawn line. On a lightly floured surface, use a floured rolling pin to roll out dough to ¼-inch thickness. Place pattern on dough and use a sharp knife to cut around pattern. Transfer cookies to a greased baking sheet. Bake 20 to 25 minutes or until light brown. Cool completely on a wire rack. Store in an airtight container.

Yield: about 1 dozen 5-inch cookies

SPICED COFFEE MIX

    4 cups firmly packed brown sugar
    2 cups coffee-flavored liqueur
    1½ cups nondairy powdered creamer
    1½ teaspoons ground cinnamon
    1 teaspoon ground allspice

In a large bowl, mix together all ingredients using lowest speed of an electric mixer. Cover and chill overnight. Store in an airtight container in refrigerator. To serve, spoon 1 tablespoon of mix into a mug. Stir in 6 ounces of desired hot beverage such as coffee, wine, cocoa, or milk.

Yield: about 4 cups of mix

A loaf of dessert bread is always a welcome gift, especially when you deliver it in a festive carrier like this Santa Basket. Drizzled with creamy frosting, Cinnamon-Banana Bread is enriched with brown sugar and pecans.

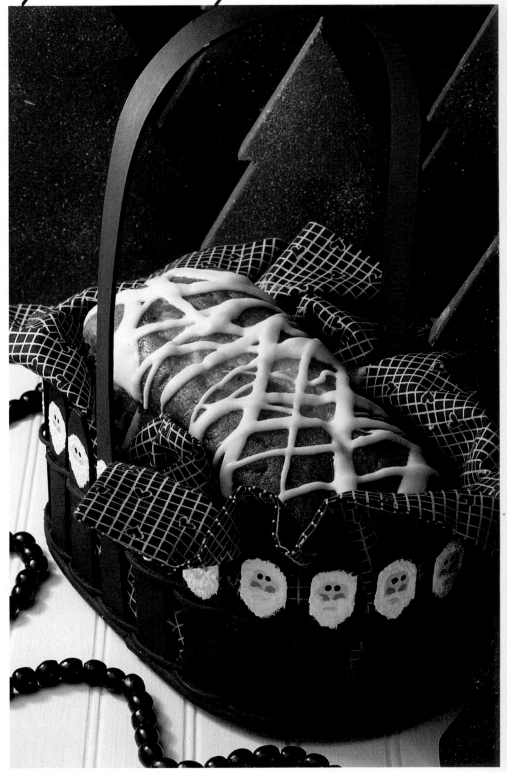

CINNAMON-BANANA BREAD

BREAD

- 1 cup firmly packed brown sugar
- 1 cup butter or margarine, divided
- 2 ripe bananas, cut into small pieces
- ½ cup chopped pecans
- ½ cup granulated sugar
- 2 eggs
- 1¾ cups all-purpose flour
- 2 tablespoons ground cinnamon
- 1 teaspoon baking powder
- ½ teaspoon baking soda

FROSTING

- 1¼ cups confectioners sugar
- 1 package (3 ounces) cream cheese, softened

Preheat oven to 350 degrees. For bread, combine brown sugar and ½ cup butter in a medium saucepan over medium heat, stirring until butter is melted. Add bananas and pecans, stirring until well coated. Cool to room temperature.

In a large bowl, cream remaining butter and granulated sugar until fluffy. Beat in eggs. In another large bowl, sift together next 4 ingredients. Mix dry ingredients into creamed mixture. Stir in banana mixture. Divide batter evenly between 2 greased 3½ x 6¾-inch loaf pans. Bake 45 to 50 minutes or until a toothpick inserted in center comes out clean. Cool in pan 10 minutes. Turn onto a wire rack to cool completely.

For frosting, combine sugar and cream cheese in a medium bowl. Using medium speed of an electric mixer, mix until smooth. Drizzle frosting over bread. Store in airtight container.

Yield: 2 loaves of bread

SANTA BASKET

You will need a basket with sides resembling a picket fence; matte red spray paint; peach, black, and pink acrylic paint; small paintbrush; small stiff paintbrush; and Duncan Snow Accents™ (available at craft stores).

1. (Note: Refer to photo to paint basket, allowing to dry between colors.) Spray paint basket red.

2. For each Santa face, paint a peach oval ½" from top of "picket"; paint eyes black and cheeks pink.

3. Use stiff brush and Snow Accents™ to paint beard and hat trim.

A "Berry" Merry Gift

A bottle of fruity Raspberry Wine is sure to be a ''berry'' merry gift. For a fun presentation, slip it into our cute Santa Wine Bag.

RASPBERRY WINE

3 cups frozen unsweetened raspberries, thawed
¼ cup granulated sugar
1 bottle (720 ml) dry white wine

In a large bowl, combine raspberries and sugar, stirring until well coated. Stir in wine until sugar is dissolved. Cover and chill 5 days. Strain wine through a fine sieve. Store in the refrigerator. Serve chilled.
Yield: about 3 cups of wine

SANTA WINE BAG

You will need one 13" x 23" piece of red fabric for bag, one 8" x 14" piece of artificial lamb fleece for beard and trim, one 4" square of flesh-colored fabric for face, one 2" dia. white pom-pom, 16" of ⅛"w red satin ribbon, red and white thread, fabric glue, tracing paper, seam ripper, one ⅜" dia. pink button, and two ⅜" dia. black buttons.

1. Use beard pattern and follow **Transferring Patterns**, page 156. Use pattern and cut beard from fleece. For trim, cut a 1" x 13" strip from fleece.
2. With 1 edge (top) of face piece 14½" from 1 short edge (top) of bag piece, center and glue face piece to right side of bag piece. Allow to dry.
3. Referring to photo and matching top edges, center and glue beard to face. With 1 long edge of trim strip and top of

face overlapping ¼", center and glue trim strip to bag piece. Allow to dry.
4. Sew black buttons to face for eyes; sew pink button to face for nose.
5. For bag, match right sides and fold bag piece in half lengthwise. Use a ½" seam allowance and sew long edges together to form a tube. Press seam open.
6. With seam at center back, press tube flat. Use a ½" seam allowance and sew raw edges together at bottom of tube.
7. Match each pressed line to seam at bottom of tube; sew across each corner 1" from end (**Fig. 1**). Turn right side out.

Fig. 1

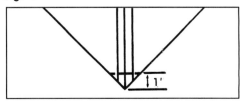

8. For casing, press remaining raw edge ¼" to wrong side; press ½" to wrong side again and stitch in place. Use seam ripper to open casing on outside of bag at seamline. Thread ribbon through casing.
9. Tack pom-pom to outside of bag below casing.

TRANSFERRING PATTERNS

When entire pattern is shown, place a piece of tracing paper over pattern and trace pattern, marking all placement symbols and markings. Cut out traced pattern.

When one-half of pattern is shown, fold tracing paper in half and place fold along dashed line of pattern. Trace pattern half, marking all placement symbols and markings; turn folded paper over and draw over all markings. Cut out traced pattern; unfold pattern and lay it flat.

SEWING SHAPES

1. Center pattern on wrong side of 1 fabric piece and use a fabric marking pencil or pen to draw around pattern. **DO NOT CUT OUT SHAPE.**
2. Place fabric pieces right sides together. Leaving an opening for turning, carefully sew pieces together **directly on pencil or pen line**.
3. Leaving a ¼ " seam allowance, cut out shape. Clip seam allowance at curves and corners. Turn shape right side out. Use the rounded end of a small crochet hook to completely turn small areas.
4. If pattern has facial features or detail lines, use fabric marking pencil or pen to lightly mark placement of features or lines.

CROSS STITCH

COUNTED CROSS STITCH

Work 1 Cross Stitch to correspond to each colored square on the chart. For horizontal rows, work stitches in 2 journeys (**Fig. 1**). For vertical rows, complete each stitch as shown in **Fig. 2**. When working over 2 fabric threads, work Cross Stitch as shown in **Fig. 3**. When the chart shows a Backstitch crossing a colored square (**Fig. 4**), a Cross Stitch (**Fig. 1, 2,** or **3**) should be worked first; then the Backstitch (**Fig. 7**) should be worked on top of the Cross Stitch.

Fig. 1

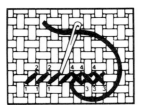

Fig. 2

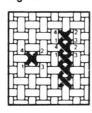

Fig. 3

Fig. 4

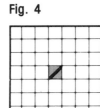

QUARTER STITCH (¼X)

Quarter Stitches are denoted by triangular shapes of color on the chart and on the color key. Come up at 1 (**Fig. 5**); then split fabric thread to go down at 2. **Fig. 6** shows this technique when working over 2 fabric threads.

Fig. 5

Fig. 6

BACKSTITCH

For outline detail, Backstitch (shown on chart and on color key by black or colored straight lines) should be worked after the design has been completed (**Fig. 7**).

Fig. 7

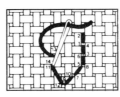

WORKING ON LINEN

Using a hoop is optional when working on linen. Roll excess fabric from left to right until stitching area is in proper position. Use the sewing method when working over 2 threads. To use the sewing method, keep your stitching hand on the right side of the fabric; take the needle down and up with 1 stroke. To add support to stitches, place the first Cross Stitch on the fabric with stitch 1-2 beginning and ending where a vertical fabric thread crosses over a horizontal fabric thread (**Fig. 8**).

Fig. 8

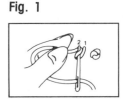

EMBROIDERY

FRENCH KNOT

Bring needle up at 1. Wrap thread once around needle and insert needle at 2, holding end of thread with non-stitching fingers (**Fig. 1**). Tighten knot; then pull needle through fabric, holding thread until it must be released. For a larger knot, use more strands; wrap only once.

Fig. 1

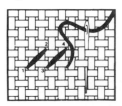

RUNNING STITCH

Make a series of straight stitches with stitch length equal to the space between stitches (**Fig. 2**).

Fig. 2

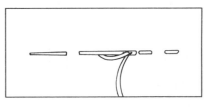

PLASTIC CANVAS

GOBELIN STITCH

This basic stitch is worked over 2 or more threads or intersections. The number of threads or intersections may vary according to the chart (**Fig. 1**).

Fig. 1

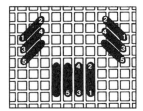

TENT STITCH

This stitch is worked in vertical or horizontal rows over 1 intersection as shown in **Fig. 2**. Follow **Fig. 3** to work Reversed Tent Stitch.

Fig. 2

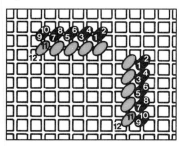

Fig. 3

OVERCAST STITCH

This stitch covers the edge of the canvas and joins pieces of canvas (**Fig. 4**). It may be necessary to go through the same hole more than once to get an even coverage on the edge, especially at the corners.

Fig. 4

CROCHET

SINGLE CROCHET

To begin a single crochet, insert hook into ridge of chain or under V of stitch. Hook yarn and draw through (**Fig. 1**). There are now 2 loops on hook (**Fig. 2**). Hook yarn and draw through the 2 loops on hook. One single crochet is now complete.

Fig. 1

Fig. 2

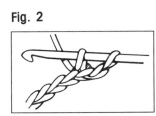

DOUBLE CROCHET

To begin a double crochet, wind yarn once over hook, bringing yarn from back over top of hook. Insert hook into ridge of chain or under V of stitch. Hook yarn and draw through. There should now be 3 loops on hook (**Fig. 3**). Hook yarn again and draw through the first 2 loops on hook (**Fig. 4**); 2 loops should remain on hook. Hook yarn again and draw through remaining 2 loops (**Fig. 5**). One double crochet is now complete.

Fig. 3

Fig. 4

Fig. 5

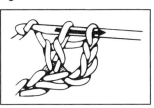

KNITTING

KNITTING

Hold the needle with the stitches in your left hand and the empty needle in your right hand. With the yarn in back of the needles, insert the right needle into the front of the stitch closest to the tip of the left needle from left to right. Bring the yarn beneath the right needle and between the needles from back to front (**Fig. 1**). Bring the right needle, with the loop of yarn, toward you and through the stitch (**Fig. 2**); slip the old stitch off the left needle.

Fig. 1

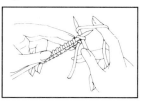

Fig. 2

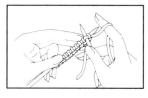

PURLING

Hold the needle with the stitches in your left hand and the empty needle in your right hand. With the yarn in front of the needles, insert the right needle into the front of the stitch closest to the tip of the left needle from right to left. Bring the yarn between the needles from right to left and around the right needle (**Fig. 3**). Move the right needle, with the loop of yarn, through the stitch and away from you (**Fig. 4**); slip the old stitch off the left needle.

Fig. 3

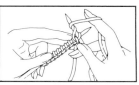

Fig. 4

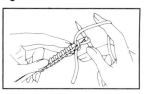

CREDITS

We want to extend a warm thank you to the generous people who allowed us to photograph our projects in their homes.

- *Winter in the Village*: Tom and Jane New
- *Christmas at Grandmother's House*: Dr. Reed and Becky Thompson
- *A Festival of Trees*: Carl and Monte Brunck, Shirley Held, and Gordon and Kelly Holt
- *I Believe*: Charles and Peg Mills
- *Fruits of the Season*: Shirley Held
- *Journey to Bethlehem*: The Clawson Family
- *A Cozy Country Christmas*: The Clawson Family

We also thank the Capital Hotel in Little Rock, Arkansas, for allowing us to photograph a portion of our *Caroling Party* section in the hotel.

We especially thank Nancy Newell for allowing us to photograph our division pages in her home, the historic Ten Mile House in Little Rock, Arkansas. The Ten Mile House hosts an annual Christmas Open House to benefit Pulaski County SCAN (Suspected Child Abuse and Neglect). We also appreciate her helpfulness and generosity in letting us use many of her antique toys.

Our heartfelt thanks is also extended to Carl and Monte Brunck for allowing us to photograph our book cover in their home.

A word of thanks goes to the Green Thumb Garden Center of Little Rock, Arkansas, for contributing the Canadian hemlock tree shown on page 39.

To Magna IV Engravers of Little Rock, Arkansas, we say thank you for the superb color reproduction and excellent pre-press preparation.

We want to especially thank photographers Ken West, Larry Pennington, and Mark Mathews of Peerless Photography, Little Rock, Arkansas, for their time, patience, and excellent work.

To the talented designers who helped in the creation of many of the projects in this book, we extend a special word of thanks.

- *Papier Mâché Star and Icicle Ornaments*, page 15, and *Papier Mâché Santa Ornaments*, page 47: Susan Brack
- *Plastic Canvas Ornaments*, page 50: Concept by Leslie T. Arens
- *Dried Apple Ornaments*, page 82: Joanna Randolph Rott
- *Rich Wrap*, page 98: Linda Gillum of Kooler Design Studio

We extend a sincere thank you to all the people who assisted in making and testing the projects in this book: Nelda Newby, Marsha White, Jennie Black, Karen Tyler, Andrea Ahlen, Vicky Bishop, Karen Brogan, Catherine Hubmann, Thelma Hyatt, Pat Johnson, Tracy Rhein, Cristel Shelton, and Chuck Tedder.

Instructions for the *Reindeer* shown on page 152 can be found in *The Spirit of Christmas, Book Three*.